And for This,
I Am Grateful

Inspirations for Caregivers
on the Alzheimer's Journey

by

Susan Vohs Fairley

Edited by

Nancy Shohet West

DEDICATION

This book is dedicated with love and gratitude
to my caregiving husband, Gary Fairley; to my
support group, Hope In the Hammock; to the
memory of my mother, Olive Young Vohs; and
to my beloved friends, Robin Sullivan and
Judy Wiginton, without whose love and support
this book would not have been possible.

FOREWORD

The journey of caring for a loved one with Alzheimer's disease is much like the wildest roller coaster ride one can imagine. There are no two journeys that are the same, as each Alzheimer patient has had a different life journey and in each individual case the mind closes down differently.

In hindsight I know there were signs that I missed or ignored. The first major sign was probably in 2006, when my 83-year-old mother told me she was getting a puppy. She had not had a dog since our childhood pet over forty years prior. The reason it was easy to dismiss this unusual decision was that mom knew exactly what kind of puppy she wanted, located the breeder, made all of the arrangements and had me drive her to see the litter two weeks after birth so she would have the best selection. She appeared to know exactly what she was doing.

I am not complaining, because Bonnie was certainly a blessing and still is today…but it was a very unusual decision that seemed to come out of the blue. The good news is that I knew

Bonnie would most likely outlive my mother, so two days later I returned to the breeder and picked out a sister. We are blessed to have both girls with us today, Bonnie and Summer.

The next big decision came in December of 2007, when my mother surprised my brother and me with the news that she planned to move to Florida when her lease was up in March. Though this was great news, as my brother and I both lived in Palm Coast, it was quite unexpected, as she had been saying for years she would never leave Georgia. We welcomed her and found a little rental home close to where my husband Gary and I live.

In retrospect, while again a blessing in disguise, the surprising decision to move to a new state seems like it might have been an early indicator of the onset of Alzheimer's disease. Even more importantly, the anxiety and nervousness that prevailed throughout her move was not typical of her personality.

Later that year, she was definitively diagnosed with Alzheimer's, a diagnosis that touched off a journey for all of us which would last for the next four years until the end of my mother's life. The Alzheimer's journey is an experience like no other that a family will ever go through. My mother's change in personality was almost unbearable for me. My father had passed away when I was fourteen – my mother was forty at the time – and as the youngest of three siblings, I was the only one still living at home. As a result, my newly widowed mother and I became fast friends. We had a loving and close relationship that lasted through the decades to come; I don't think that there were more than a few days in my entire adult life that we didn't speak on the phone. We didn't always agree; we didn't always get along perfectly; but we were always loving and closely attached to one another.

So the hostility that accompanies Alzheimer's in some patients was a particularly painful blow to me, as was the irrational behavior that went with it. We went through many stages with her, some excruciatingly difficult. First my mother was living on her own just a street away from my husband and me; then she moved into our house; then we had to move her to an assisted living facility.

At a particularly challenging time, I decided to seek out a support group. I found one, but somehow it didn't really seem to give me quite what I needed. I still felt there was no one knowledgeable and supportive to whom I could unburden myself. My husband Gary was wonderful both with me and with my mother, but this was all new to him as well; we were growing together in our understanding of Alzheimer's, but he couldn't serve as a source of knowledge for me. That was what I needed, people on the same journey but with more experience and insights than I had.

Two practices that did help me during that time were yoga and long walks by the ocean. Those were my primary means of self-care, and they served as positive forces in my life. But then something even more positive transpired. Not long before my mother died in 2012, a casual friend named Gail from my yoga class asked me to read a book called "Make Miracles in 40 Days" by Melody Beattie. I have to confess that reading had become difficult for me; I just didn't have the concentration while I was so distracted with my mother's care.

But with Gail's encouragement, I picked up the book and started reading it anyway, and then something happened unrelated to my mother's care that did seem like a miracle. My husband and I volunteer as guardians ad litem, which means we help make decisions for juveniles who are wards of the state. A serious problem had befallen one of the kids in our care. Inspired somehow by the book, I picked up the phone despite the fact that it was a Saturday afternoon on a holiday weekend and placed a call to the head of the guardian ad litem program for the entire state of Florida. To my amazement, he answered the phone. He listened to my concern. And we were able to make a decision that saved this young person's life.

At that point, I was sold on the value of the miracles book. I called Gail and said, "I'm in."

The book asks you to make a forty-day commitment to writing down your gratitude every day and send it to your chosen gratitude partner. Gail and I started the habit then and have maintained it ever since. And both of us have seen an amazing number of miracles transpire in our lives during that time.

Not long after that, my mother passed away. I continued with yoga and daily gratitudes, and then one day an acquaintance contacted me to say she had a friend who was struggling to care for her husband with Alzheimer's. I agreed that maybe my experience could be helpful, so I emailed her friend, whose name was Margo Usher. We began exchanging regular emails and then we started meeting once a month for lunch. Drawing on my experience with my mother, I tried to provide help, sympathy and support as Margo faced difficult milestones such as moving her husband to assisted living.

Then the same acquaintance that put me in touch with Margo contacted me again and said she had another friend who could use my help: Robin Sullivan, who was caring for her mother with Alzheimer's. Robin joined up with Margo and me, and the three of us formed a regular support group.

With my mother gone, I thought that maybe I could reach out to still more people. I approached Margo and Robin to see if they would consider helping me start a more public support group. I was certain they'd say no. Robin's mother and Margo's husband were both still living at that time, and I was sure they wouldn't want to take on any new responsibilities. But to my surprise, these two brave and wonderful ladies said yes!

So that's how the group, Hope In the Hammock, began. Robin and Margo got permission from their local church for us to hold meetings there and spread the word among their friends; I mentioned it to my yoga class. About 8-12 of us were soon meeting monthly. And then at some point I began emailing the group every Sunday to offer words of inspiration and encouragement. The email list grew rapidly as members forwarded it to friends.

What always surprises me is that I wake up every Sunday with no idea of what I'm going to write that day, and yet somehow as soon as I sit down at my computer, the words begin to flow. So much piques my interest and seems to be connected to the Alzheimer's journey: nature – whether in the form of a beautiful sunrise or a massively destructive hurricane – holidays, pets, friends, prayers, anniversaries, grandchildren, travel, random memories of my mother. I've even written about the Super Bowl!

The network of support that has resulted from the newsletter is simply amazing to me. I hear back from readers all the way from Florida to Pittsburgh and beyond. Some people write to me with very detailed accounts of their own situation; others just say "Thank you" or "That was very meaningful to me."

What I always think about is that as difficult as it was for me to care for my mother, I owe all of this to her. This support network all began from my experience as her caregiver. And it has brought me so much joy. When I started out caring for my mother, I needed support that I could not find. Now, along with my friends, I'm providing that needed support for other people. That's a wonderful feeling. It really reflects how much help people find in each other. Group members come and go. We laugh and cry together. I witness firsthand that we are meeting a critical need that all caregivers have for sustenance and empathy.

Now that I'm battling cancer, I can no longer attend the group regularly anymore. But I'm so grateful that they've stayed together, and I write the weekly newsletter no matter how I'm feeling. Whatever I find to write, it never feels like a waste of time. I've come to realize that if I am able to connect emotionally with even one person in what I write, it was worth every minute of time and effort. I may be providing support and inspiration to others, but at the same time, they are sending all those good feelings right back to me.

And for this, I'm grateful…grateful to my mother, and grateful to Alzheimer's. It has brought me a loving, supportive community and a way for me to give back. What a blessing.

Susan Vohs Fairley

Palm Coast, Florida
March 2017

Author's Note to Readers

I just wanted to share a short note about the use of this book. These are WEEKLY inspirations and they are not to be read all at once or even daily. You need to take time to read the message and then close your eyes and just breathe. Let the words penetrate. You may want to reread the message once or twice during the week, even possibly share it with a friend. At the end of the week take a moment to reflect and see if anything changed during your week. Hopefully you will notice something, despite how small it might seem. My hope is that there is at least one thing that will be helpful to you during your journey.

Remember you are not alone. I truly suggest you seek out a support group or at least one close friend who will be nothing but a wonderful listener and shoulder to lean on.

I also suggest you look for a Walk to End Alzheimer's in your area (go to www.ALZ.org). Becoming a team member or starting a team of your own is very empowering.

Good luck, my friend, and please feel free to contact me at fairleysv2016@gmail.com. Just be sure to put "And for this I am grateful" in the subject line.

I hope this book is of some help and support to you.

Sincerely,

Susan Fairley

Happy New Year, my wonderful Care Givers!

I hope the last evening of the year was just what you wanted it to be...peaceful, joyful, quiet...whatever you needed and wished the end of the year to look like. But if not, this is the perfect morning to ...LET IT GO!

New Year's Day is a great reminder for the ALZ caregiver, as it not only on New Year's Day, but every day and every moment...that we have to let it go...forget what lies behind...for if you don't...you may just very well miss the best moment ever.

Letting go sounds so simple, I know it isn't...however, it may be one of the best lessons to take away from the ALZ journey. There were times I so wanted to stay angry with my mother and to hold onto the hurt from the words she spewed, to make my decisions about her life journey out of anger...and then in an instant she made me laugh and I could remember our life journey of love and friendship. Had I not been able to let it go...I would not have those loving memories today. Trust me...it was not always easy...I walked many a mile along our shores praying for strength and compassion to let it go...and when I did...I could see so much clearer and appreciate so much more.

Today I realize how blessed I was. I had loving memories to look back upon, to remember from long ago. Not everyone is so blessed. Not every caregiver can look back to beautiful memories but needs to draw upon their faith in what is right and just. Whichever is your case, let go of the pain and look forward to the small moments of love and compassion. Know that at the end of this journey you will have wonderful moments of gratitude for the love and compassion you showed during this most difficult journey.

Take a moment to thank the people around you who are helping you through this journey: a spouse, a child, a friend, whoever it is that is giving you strength to breathe, to laugh, to LET IT GO!

I am so GRATEFUL for my husband, without him I would have felt completely alone in my journey with mom and ALZ. He endured more than a son-in-law should have to endure. I could not have made it without him dancing mom out of the bathroom and on the count of three tossing her into bed...what a great memory...now...thank God I had Gary to help me laugh when I was about to crash!

Take a look around this morning, this new day, this new year, and be grateful for those who love you during this journey in life. See the miracles God has set in your path to help you LET IT GO and appreciate what is.

So, one year is gone and a New Year has arrived. Cherish the good moments, let go of the others...remember...there are no mistakes...only the best decisions we knew how to make at that moment in time. If a decision does not look or feel the way you thought it would, remember that you made the best decision you knew how to make...learn from it and move forward...that is what makes life so wonderful....the present!

Much Love my Friends,

Me

Happy New Year!

Good Morning My Fabulous Caregivers,

Today is Sunday and tomorrow we meet! I am so grateful that we will all be together once again to share, to laugh, to cry, to pray, to support, in whatever manner is needed.

We are ten days into our new year. It is difficult to believe that so much can change and happen in just ten days, but it is a new chapter in your book, the ALZ Journey, and we will be together to begin your next chapter.

I love the opening of my inspirational reading this morning... *"Wherever you have been, and whatever you have done so far, your entire life was building up to this moment. Now is your time to burst into your greatness, a greatness you could never achieve without going through exactly the things you have gone through."* Tomorrow morning, come open to hear God whisper to you...or He may just have to shout...but be open to hear Him tell you of the Greatness you are about to achieve. Don't you think that is why He has brought us all together?...He knows we hear better when there are more ears to listen...I sure think so; it is most definitely not by chance.

Hugs my fabulous caregivers...I cannot wait to see you tomorrow. Remember everyone is welcome. It would be wonderful to begin the New Year with New Friends.
Remember YOU are absolutely the BEST!
Me

GM My Wonderful Care Giving Friends,

Can you believe the first two weeks of the New Year are already over? Amazing truly, and even more amazing is all that has transpired in just a few weeks. That is how I think of the advocate/caregiving journey, so amazing what transpires in a short time. No wonder we are exhausted and yet in so many ways grateful for those memories.

In one week two friends who have battled illness for quite some time have passed forward to a peaceful, healthy beginning. While they will be missed, there is not a friend or family member who is not grateful for their peace and the peace and much-needed rest of their spouse and loving caregiver.

My friend Joanne had just recently placed her husband in a VA home. I was so worried she might have some regrets after years of caregiving, that this was her final decision. I loved what she said. "No regrets, for the first time in years I was rested and able to totally enjoy my visits with Ed. I saw him every day, it was not perfect, but it was far from perfect at home. What was much better, I was rested, and relaxed enough to sit patiently, hold his hand and just chat. I was able to let go of what I could not change and just enjoy the love we had shared for over fifty years."

It took a loving and capable nurse to say... "Joanne, do not worry about his medication schedule, Ed no longer needs to take those medications, what he needs is for you to just hold his hand and enjoy his final journey." Enjoy the final journey...wow...so grateful she was able to do this.

The journey of ALZ is a bit like this week's weather. Some days are beautiful with warm sunshine and calm seas, the next day is filled with a beautiful rain giving our trees and grass a fresh drink which was so needed after Hurricane Matthew and now, gray skies, rolling waves and cold temperatures. We have gone from shorts to sweatshirts in just one week. We need it all, but it can be exhausting and overwhelming when you wake up each morning and have no idea what the weather will bring.

We can't change the weather and amazingly we don't seem to try. So during your caregiving journey, take what comes, enjoy the journey as much as possible, accept that there will be stormy days and huge changes, make the best decision you can for the moment...no regrets. If you get outside and it is colder than you thought...just go in and put on another layer...find the silver lining of the moment and adjust your decisions based on what you know

now. Maya Angelou said, "I did then what I knew how to do. Now that I know better I do better." That is the best any of us can do.

Rest in peace to Ed and Harold. I am so grateful Joanne and Sara took time to allow themselves to enjoy their final journey together.

Hugs my friends, do what you know best to do and enjoy the journey, the sun will come out tomorrow.

Love you,

Me

GM My Wonderful Care Giving Advocates,

Happy Sunday! We have a new person to welcome. Rita hopes to join us for our next support group meeting. Welcome Rita, we look forward to meeting you.

It is always amazing to me how much transpires in one short week. But this is much like the journey of ALZ...amazing, really. We have had beautiful weather, rain, a gorgeous full moon, gentle lapping waves, to crashing waves, high tides and low tides, fog, cloudy skies, gentle sunrises and sunsets, warm temps and cool temps...changes every day and sometimes several in a day. Yet, during most weather-related and Mother Nature-related cases, we do not get upset. We let it go and just enjoy the journey. Why? Because we know it is out of our control and for me personally, I know God has this!

Doesn't the weather remind you of the journey of caregiving for a loved one with ALZ. There are those moments filled with sunshine and laughter and in just a moment, with no notice, an event that can bring us to tears. There are days filled with gentle lapping waves and nights filled with waves crashing all around us. There are days that we are sure the worst is over, only for a new adventure the following week. Yet, for some reason when it comes to ALZ and our loved ones, it is more difficult for us to let it go and let God. Why is that? Do we believe we are in control of this disease? Of the day's events? Of our loved one? Today, this new day, I just want to remind you to let it GO. We are not in control; God is. We cannot control the journey; all we can simply do is make it as peaceful as possible.

How, you might ask? Remember, it is a disease. You cannot cure it. Remember that you are not in control; God is. Remember, your sole duty as a care giver is to be as loving as humanly possible, no arguing, no disagreeing, just loving and letting it go. It is not personal and it is not about you.

Will there be moments you want to scream? Yes. Will there be moments you want to laugh out loud? Yes. Will there be moments you want to cry? Yes. Will there be moments you wonder why? Yes. But just breathe and let it go. The next moment is a brand new moment and it could be the most wonderful moment of the journey. You do not want to miss it.

So my friends, it is a new week, and yes, there will be ups and downs. Let's promise each other to smile through them, to breathe. That is all we can do, because we are not in control. Yes, it is true, it does help to scream every now and then, or cry and wash away the sadness of the journey, but once that is over...let it go! Do you think that song from "Frozen" was written for us? Maybe!

We are not in control. Let He who is in control hold your hand, lift you up and carry you through...truthfully that is all we can do...so no reason to fight it. Seek the support of loved ones, of us, you are not alone. Not only are we with you, but God has your back, all the time!

Love you my friends, today begins a new day, a new week and a new journey in time...enjoy it.

Me

GM My sweet, Care Giving Advocates,

Happy Sunday! I apologize that I am late with this morning's message, but I am a bit under the weather and the girls wanted to snuggle a little longer...I took advantage of that wonderful luxury. ☺

Carolyn is my inspiration this morning...she is so brave and reflective. There comes a time for all of us when we know we cannot do it alone. Even with God by our side, the time comes when we need physical help. I am so grateful that God is there to guide us to this decision and grateful when I see someone listen...(before they have a brick dropped on their head.) ☺ I am sad to say that often times God has to do more than give me a nudge...He has to practically roll me off a cliff. Grateful for those who listen to gentle whispers.

I vividly remember while walking the ALZ journey with mother, talking with my niece who had a two-year-old at the time. She would call to tell me a struggle that she had that day and I would say…That is so funny, I had that same struggle with mother today. Yes, during this journey, the time comes when we cannot allow our loved ones to be in charge of decisions, we must be the decision-makers for them…much like a parent of a young child. It is not mean; it is loving. We care too much to allow them to get hurt.

I believe one of the most difficult parts of the ALZ journey is that there are times that we see a capable person, we see someone who believes they are capable of making sound decisions. At those moments it becomes easy to convince ourselves that they will be OK, that they can drive, or stay by themselves, or they are right to get angry if we need extra help. But the truth is, this disease robs them of this ability and we have to stay strong in our decision-making… not only for them but for ourselves. They will adjust like our children adjust to our rules. They may get upset, they may pout, but in truth they will eventually accept the decision.

So Carolyn, my hat is off to you my friend. You are making those difficult decisions. You are seeking help from your support group and we all say…Yes…do what needs to be done. Charlie can no longer make the decisions. We support you 100%. If this new caregiver has problems and Linda had problems…then we know who is really struggling with the situation…Charlie.

My mother liked only one caregiver…the one who came first thing in the morning when she was freshest. The problem was we had three caregivers. While I will say she never had a warm and fuzzy relationship with the other two...she adjusted. I often said, mom, I am so sorry, but this is who is available to stay with you while I run errands, please be nice to them. Sometimes that worked...sometimes it did NOT! But they stayed and we survived.

Remember...you are making the best decision you know how to make at this point in time...it is the correct decision. You are doing what is best for your loved one...caring for the caregiver while caring for the patient.

Thank you Carolyn for being my inspiration this morning. We are all praying that all goes well. I only know one thing...YOU are doing the best that you know how and that is all you can do! Hugs and have a wonderful week, everyone.

Me

GM My Wonderful Care Giving Advocates and Friends,

It is not every day in FL that we can think Hot Chocolate...but this is one of those mornings...so this morning I wish you a Cup of Hot Chocolate!

I can hardly believe that this is our last Sunday in January. That means that this New Year is moving forward...ready or not!

I stopped to read an e-mail this morning, something I do not normally do before writing, but as you know there is always a reason for the things we do...I needed to read that e-mail. It was truthfully a little story about entering heaven, and considering I was asked yesterday what I expect to see when my time comes, it piqued my interest.

The Angel was showing our group around and he brought us to the receiving room. This room was busy with angels everywhere receiving requests from earth...reading each one carefully...while the room was filled with angels they could barely keep up. Those Prayer Warriors can keep things pretty busy!

The next room was the processing room and it too was filled with busy angels trying to package and process all of the requests and return them to earth as promptly as possible. Once again filled with angels working as fast as possible, it was difficult to keep up with so many requests to grant.

The final room was the acknowledgement room. In this room there was one lonely angel with nothing to do. How can this be possible, we asked. The angel said, people forget when they have been acknowledged their requests to say... thank you. One brave member of our group asked...but how do you thank God for all that He does and the angel replied...simply say... Thank You God!

So I guess the reason I stopped to read that this morning is because in truth, it is sometimes very difficult to see while walking the ALZ journey that God is still acknowledging our requests. He is still there. No, He will not remove the ALZ for us, but He is there to walk us through the journey. He is there to nudge us through the difficult decisions, to hear our pleas of what to do next. And all we need to say is...Thank you God.

I recall my first miracle during the ALZ journey. My mother was coming home from rehab with many new needs. I had no nursing experience, no one to call for help, a bathroom that was definitely not going to work for her and a weekend to get ready. I remember looking out our front window and simply saying... Dear God please help us. (I am not even sure this was a prayer or simply a desperate thought.) Regardless, the angels grabbed it up and forwarded it to the processing room. And in that moment I saw my neighbor's contractor. I walked over and asked if he could help...over the weekend he and his partner pulled out our tub and re-installed a shower. I then saw my other neighbor push her mother's wheelchair to the car...I went over and asked...do you have the number of anyone I can call for help? She said, yes, call this lady. I did and on Monday I had three angels lined up that became my mother's helpers for the time she was here. I was never so grateful. To some it may seem like a coincidence and therefore simply forget to say Thank You. But we know He is with us always. You are never alone.

Be strong, my friends...so it is cool outside...there is no snow ...the sun will shine and you can enjoy a cup of hot chocolate. So be grateful!

What can you say... "Thank You God" for this morning? Start your week off with gratitude from the journey. There is a silver lining in every journey, we just sometimes take them for granted. This past week I was accepted into the Cancer Research Trial...not a really fun process I might add...but I am so grateful to have these miracle pills to take. Thank You Jesus!

Have a wonderful day, a grateful week, and we will soon be together. See you then.

Much Love and Gratitude,

Me

GM My wonderful Care Giving Advocates,

It seems that I am blessed to write you on some pretty wonderful days. Not only is it the first Sunday in February, but it is also Super Bowl Sunday. Today our Atlanta Falcons are playing and we are pretty excited. It has been a long time coming. Believe it or not, the road to the Super Bowl is much like the journey of dementia...filled with ups and downs, good times and bad times, but it is YOU, the loyal fan, who is there to the very end.

So this morning I am going to reflect on the Super Bowl journey and hopefully you will see the connection to your caregiving journey. It has been 18 years since the Falcons went to the Super Bowl; in 51 years, they have never won a Super Bowl. Coaches have come and gone, players have come and gone and now here they are back in the Super Bowl with a chance to win...an opportunity of a lifetime.

The journey has not been easy. Stadiums changed, players changed, fans changed, truthfully the entire playing field has changed since the original Falcons team began in 1966. But today they have the opportunity to win and win big. There are some fans who have NEVER given up hope for this day and they never will. They will be loyal fans until the very end.

It is so amazing to me how many of life's journeys are connected. Today, you are the #1 Loyal Fan. You have been there from the beginning and you have held on to HOPE during every single game and season. You have never stopped CHEERING or LOVING your team. The coach changed, the stadium changed, the players have even changed...but you remain the #1 Loyal Fan. You have been there and will be there until your team throws the final pass, in the final game. You will HOPE for a victory but it may not be today. You may get really angry and hurt if they lose today, after all you have been LOYAL and FAITHFUL all this time. But in truth, once you take that deep breath and just let your LOVE wash over you, you know you will once again be the #1 FAN. You will be there until the game is over and for the next season. You may enjoy a win or perhaps you may never see that day, but regardless of the outcome of this day, you will have forever been the #1 FAN. And that my friend is what makes you so GREAT!

Because no matter what has happened or what happens today...YOU will let it go and remain the #1 FAN! It does not matter where your loved one is, or how they play today, all that matters is that they are your TEAM and you are their #1 FAN.

So my friends cheer on, take that deep breath and HOPE for the best. Regardless of what happens today, this is your TEAM and you are their ADVOCATE...not the coach, not the playing field, not even a team member...you are even GREATER...you are the #1 FAN... without you, there is no SUPER BOWL!

Thank you for your LOYALTY, for your HOPE, for your CHEERS, for your BELIEF...YOU are the #1 FAN who remains until the very end of the GAME!

Hugs, my friends, enjoy this day.

Me

My dear Susan,
You have given me the strength to travel on this journey. You have told me funny stories that you had with your Mom that I laugh about as similar things happen to us. I know you were sent to me by our Father in Heaven. Thank you for being a good friend.
With God's Blessings and my love,
– Carolyn Hoffman

GM My sweet Care Givers,

Happy Valentine's Week. I am so grateful some of us will be together tomorrow. So looking forward to sharing hugs.

So in honor of Valentine's Day my thought for this week is Holding Hands. Do you remember when Fireworks is what you expected with LOVE and sometimes it was actually there...ahhh ...youth! Today my idea of real love is holding hands.

The change from Fireworks to Holding Hands is much like the journey of ALZ. Sometimes the world around them is lit up with fireworks and all they want is someone to gently hold their hand.

So this week, in honor of Valentine's Day keep everything simple. Hold hands, rub a back, hug, smile a lot, laugh, put on some romantic love songs from long ago and don't expect fireworks.

21

Now the question is ...do you do that for your loved one...or do you do it for yourself? And the answer is...BOTH!

Love you Guys, Happy Almost Valentine's Day!

See you tomorrow...

Me

GM My Beautiful Care Taking Advocates,

I apologize that I am a bit late...but on Sunday I was thinking my thought for the week would be...the Difference a Day Can Make. And yes it can, especially when it comes to illness and ALZ.

Yesterday morning I woke to two munchkins walking up the stairs to say good morning, their parents still happily in bed. ☺ This morning we are alone.

Yesterday I woke to excruciating pain that I had been in truly for over a week and a half. This morning it is in half.

Yesterday the sunrise was very gentle. This morning it is a bit more vivid, though still gentle.

Yesterday the seas were very calm, today they are calm with a few more lapping waves.

23

Yesterday Gary made a phone call to my Dr., we left home at 10:00 to meet with him. We ended up in the ER and arrived home at 10:00 last night. This morning we have to make that same phone call...I am praying that this day will make a difference in the outcome.

When I left yesterday I weighed 133 lbs. This morning I weigh 127 lbs.

Yesterday I had 31/2 liters of fluid in one side of my stomach. Today it is gone.

I could continue on...but I think you can see ...The Difference A Day Can Make. And so it is with the journey of ALZ. One day there is great confusion and the next day it appears to be gone. One day the patient is distrusting of the caregiver, the next day they have forgotten the distrust. One day they mix up their days and nights and the next they have it straight. One day they are argumentative and defiant, the next day they are not. The real difference with ALZ and other diseases...it soon changes from ...The Difference a Day Can Make...to the difference a few hours can make. It progresses. You do not know when it will be more than a day, you do not know when it will be less than a few hours, but what you do know is those symptoms, those signs of ALZ will only progress.

What does that mean to you my loving Care Givers? Work with this MOMENT in time. Enjoy the good moments and there will be some every single day. Stick those deep into your heart...even write them down... so you will not forget those most cherishable moments. Get plenty of rest by leaning on others and taking time to nourish you heart and soul so that when those difficult times arrive you are prepared to be as loving and calm as you possibly can be. And of course always pray for the strength, love and compassion that you will need to be the loving caregiver you intend to be.

What a Difference A Day Can Make...from exhaustion to a day of much-needed rest...from the most loving moment to the most difficult moment... From anxiety, to mistrust, to anger, to wandering, to forgetting the most common of tasks...to the most wonderful memory you will ever have...That is the Difference A Day Will Make.

Enjoy this day my dear friends, one moment at a time. That is what I am doing...so worry not. While my journey is not ALZ, and I am grateful for that, my Care Giver, my husband, is the loving Care Giver you are and I am so grateful. While your loved one may not be able to express that, I am expressing it for them...YOU MAKE OUR DAY EVERY DAY!

I love you all and hope to be here next Sunday...but if not...you now know The Difference a Day Can Make.

Many hugs, gratitude and much love to you all,

Me

GM My Kind, Loving, and Compassionate Caregivers,

This last Sunday in the "month of love" ... Love and Compassion... are the words that come to mind. Those two things make the difference in a caregiver. As I am ever so grateful to watch the sunrise in beautiful shades of orange and yellow over our deep blue ocean this morning, I am also grateful to know that I have experienced those two things...love and compassion.

While life is filled with unexpected journeys, ALZ/Dementia being one of them, somehow we learn to ride the tide. And I believe those of us who survive the wild ride of the tide's up and down motion are able to do so because of love and compassion.

Now that I have shared how important those two words are to this journey of Care Giving, let me say there were times my compassion was low on energy. There were times I even doubted the love I knew to be so real, and during those times I felt anger and frustration and that could lead to most anywhere, except being the best Care Giver possible.

Yes, you will run low. Refuel. Yes, you will wonder why? Refuel. Remember to smell the flowers each morning...even if it is one lonely hibiscus. Remember to say I love you with a sweet kiss, despite who greets you. Take time to hold hands and just breathe. Enjoy the music, smile and remind yourself that you are a Loving and Compassionate Care Giver and you then will know the difference that you make.

So very grateful for Love and Compassion and so is your loved one.

Miss you all, mark your calendar for our next gathering. Love you,

Me

GM My sweet and Loving Care Givers,

Here we are in March, the first Sunday of the month and the beginning of the Lenten Season. Where does the time go?

This time of year brings back so many childhood memories: hot cross buns at Publix and all the local bakeries, tulips in bloom, signs of spring around every corner and for many of us LENT...a time to make a sacrifice...to fast. Most of you most likely quickly gave up something worthwhile, but I am sure I am not the only one whose mother had to say...Really Susan, cooked carrots, I did not think you liked them so much...do you think that would be much of a sacrifice? And so it went until I finally came up with something that really made a difference to me, that made me think about each day the sacrifices that had been made for me so that I could enjoy that the other 325 days of the year. And now what we wouldn't give for our loved ones to be able to give up one or two simple things they love, but instead they have already given up so much.

So this year I am asking you to let me be your advocate, this year give up one little task that will make your day a little easier. Something that might be difficult to let go of, because you feel guilty, or the need, or it is your duty or your responsibility. Is there someone you can pass that task to for at least 40 days, to give yourself a much-needed break? Perhaps it is preparing a meal...could another caregiver do that for you once a day, once a week? Laundry? A complete day off once a week?

What is it that is such a challenge to let go, yet would truly be a blessing to you and your loved one for at least the next 40 days? A full night's sleep every week? As your advocate, I ask you to use this time to do something that will help you to be a better Care Giver in the journey. It is a long journey and this is both a sacrifice and a gift to you and your loved one.

I see Lent in a totally different light this year. So many things I enjoyed and cherished are no longer a part of my life; I have already given them up. This year I am going to be grateful for the things I can still enjoy: the blue skies, the rolling seas, my loved ones all around, the girls (our dogs). Perhaps our daily gratitude will be our new Lenten promise, being grateful for what we can still enjoy and what our loved ones can still enjoy. Take a moment this morning and thank God for all that you have and all that you were able to enjoy for so very long. While it is truly a sacrifice to give up these things we have loved, we are still blessed to have so much more.

Much love, Happy Spring, Daily Gratitude for all YOU do,
Me

GM My wonderful CareGivers:

I hope that you remembered to Spring Ahead with your time. Isn't that amazing...the push of a button and we are in a new time...we give up an hour...so that we can gain an hour later in our lives. But the joy will be with longer days and more time to see the beauty of the day. Our girls (the dogs) will be so grateful that they are getting to eat an hour earlier...but they never do adjust to the reverse. Their internal clocks just do not understand the change in time...when it is time to eat...it is time to eat. 😊 I wonder if this might be true for our loved ones? Do not be surprised if it takes them some time to adjust to the new time.

So, here we are at the beginning of a new week, a new time and this morning I am thinking about LOVE. That is my word for today. Because, as they say, it is "LOVE that makes the world go 'round!" It is your LOVE that makes you the caregiver you are. It is your LOVE that keeps you focused on what is best for your loved one. And according to my inspirational reading this morning... "it is the power of LOVE that delivers us from fear." Isn't that so true, when we feel LOVED and when we share our

LOVE we feel empowered... as if we can handle anything. And in fact we do.

So this morning, my dear friends, I wish you LOVE...because LOVE will carry you through. Let your LOVE shine and watch the LOVE return to you. Look for that smile, that moment of recognition and feel the LOVE that you share in every moment of every day. LOVE is far more enjoyable than fear or anger....so feel the LOVE.

See you tomorrow morning. I cannot wait to share my LOVE for you. You are so wonderful and I LOVE and am GRATEFUL for each and every one of you.

May the "Luck of the Irish" be ever-present with you and your LOVED ones.

Me

> *As soon as I met this group of incredible women, Robin and Susan most of all, the immediate warmth and love I received was overwhelming.*
>
> *Susan and her heartwarming Sunday morning comforts speak to my very core and have helped in dealing with my Mom more than mere words can express.*
>
> *Susan is a bright shining star in everyday life. My heart is with her and her family.*
>
> *The love I feel for her and our amazing group of ladies, Hope in the Hammock, has brought me immense joy.*
> *– Monika Karlik*

GM Sweet Care Givers,

Here we are the middle of the month...almost spring...and setting our clocks ahead one hour. It takes time to adjust to this change and we find it takes longer for our girls to adjust because they just know what time they always get up and what time they always eat and they really do not understand the time change. This could be true for your loved one and it could take some time adjusting to the change in time. So we try to phase it in with the girls...changing their eating time slowly but steadily. While I know the time change is supposed to be for energy conservation, perhaps it is also a lesson to all of us on the ALZ journey.

SLOW AND STEADY wins the race. ☺ Have you noticed that? There is no hurrying an ALZ patient, there is no quick fix, it is just slow and steady, one moment, one day at a time.

32

So perhaps we take this time change as a gentle reminder...patience above all else. When it feels as if you cannot move forward...take that moment to just breathe...to say a little prayer...to just be. When you have heard it before...just listen...shut your eyes for a brief moment and just smile... the time will come when you wish you could hear that story one more time...I promise...or even better...you will hear yourself telling the story. ☺

So the girls are still in bed...they never stay in bed until 7:00, but there they are sound asleep. Breakfast will be late but they won't know for days. Enjoy the slow and steady change of pace. Confusion may come, but remember, it will pass, and SLOW AND STEADY wins the race.

Be grateful for the moment. While there are many things I am missing, like a cup of coffee in the morning, I am more grateful for the things that I can still enjoy. I am especially grateful that I have a loving caregiver for a husband. I am grateful I can thank him a thousand times a day. While mom could not express her gratitude with words we often caught it in her smile or the look in her eyes...SLOW AND STEADY... and you will see the gratitude as well.

Hugs my friends, enjoy the time change...see what you can see differently.

Much Love and Gratitude for each one of you.

Me

GM My Sweet Caring Advocates,

Here it is a new day, a new week and the last day of WINTER! We can feel spring around the corner. Lovely! With all of that on the horizon two words come to mind...I AGREE!

Sometimes those can be extremely difficult words, but during the ALZ journey they can be our very best friends. It doesn't have to be exactly...I agree...but Yes or Sure or No Problem all come to mind. Whatever words fit the situation to keep the peace. That is our role as caregiver. This is no time to be RIGHT, but the time to be most agreeable. It is easiest when we remind ourselves it is not our loved one but the disease that may be a bit argumentative on this beautiful day. Just like Winter...let it go!

A friend once said to me, "I realize I have to change the way I respond." This is so true. The ALZ/Dementia person is going to change, but not on their own terms, so we, the caregivers, have to adapt to what they need. As they begin to misplace things, there is no need to show them the errors of their ways, just find it and give it to them. When you are accused of hiding or taking, again, oh I am so sorry, here it is. You do not have to accept the blame, but in truth just let it go, no discussion needed.

This is the perfect day to make your Spring Cleaning plans. Wash away the winter blues and let your love shine throughout spring with the most agreeable smile you can find. You will find life to be much calmer when everyone can just agree to agree:-)

Dear Lord, Give me grace to accept with serenity the things that cannot be changed,

Courage to change the things that should be changed, and the wisdom to know the difference.

Good bye Winter, hello Spring. Let your love shine through my friends.

Many hugs and much gratitude for each and every one of you.

Me

Good Morning My Beautiful Caregivers,

Today is Sunday, a new day, a new week and SPRING! The season of hope and rebirth! Spring for me is a joyful and beautiful season. Once the pollen disappears we are blessed with all the beauty of new life....birds chirping, flowers blooming, baby animals everywhere. The turtles have hatched, the whale calves have gone back home and we are here to enjoy the beauty of spring. So grateful for this new day and for you.

This morning my thoughts go straight to you...the caregiver! Sometimes when we are on the journey of caregiving we can see only our exhaustion and frustration, even what we perceive to be inadequacies linger in front of us for a while. But what I see is the most caring and loving person in the world. The person who gives of themselves unconditionally, with love and compassion. The person who wakes up and chooses to make it a good day...not just for themselves... but for whoever enters their world on this given day. You are truly a "Wonderful Person."

36

A friend shared this with me and I believe it is something I need to share with you today, the beginning of SPRING!

"It takes someone special to do what you do.

It takes someone rare and remarkable to make the lives of everyone around them nicer, brighter, and more beautiful.

It takes someone who has a big heart and a caring soul.

It takes someone who's living proof of how precious a person can be.

It take someone...just like you."

So my dear friends, Happy Spring and Thank You for being that someone special, that wonderful caregiver who does it from love and compassion, from the heart. I promise your light is shining through. You are a WONDERFUL PERSON! Take a moment right now to love yourself for all you do...a big hug would probably feel just about perfect.

Hugs my friend,

Me

GM My Wonderful Care Givers:

Here we are in the middle of March Madness, the last Sunday of the month and the only word that I can possibly share today is MIRACLE. I wear a bracelet that reads... "I believe in the possibility of a miracle everyday." But I must admit there are days, and certainly many days during my journey with ALZ, that despite my belief the word MIRACLE did not resonate in my head. But this week, I know that meaning of MIRACLE full sale. What I have discovered is that MIRACLES look totally different every day and we just have to be receptive to their appearance.

This week was my chemo free week, so I just knew Tuesday was going to be a great day. Well it wasn't that wonderful to tell you the truth...but today I can report the miracle of all miracles, I have been nauseous free for two full days! Trust me on this, I never would have believed that being nauseous free would be a miracle...but it is...and I am so grateful.

So, what I want you to think about this week while you are looking for a simple miracle...it may not look at all like you expect it to look. The ALZ journey is not going away, the outbursts will most likely continue, you are going to be frustrated, you will feel exhausted and even wonder if you can go on. But if you stop and just take a deep breath, close your eyes and say a little prayer, you will feel the MIRACLE of the moment...if nothing else that MIRACLE is knowing you are not ALONE. WE are here for you, God has you by the hand, there will be a smile, a friend, a note, a text... something that let's you know you are loved. That is the MIRACLE of the day. Savor it, breathe it in and enjoy. Tomorrow it could be a hibiscus on a bush, or a butterfly in the air, or even eating roast potatoes for the first time in months.

I believe in the possibility of a miracle everyday...I just need to pay attention to the little things in life.

May you find your MIRACLE today.

Much Love my Friends, enjoy this last week of March, and keep your eyes and heart open to the simple MIRACLE of today.
Me

Good Morning All,

It is two weeks since we were last together and so much can happen during that time. I am hoping that this finds all of you having a good day.

On the Alz.org website you can locate the Seven Stages of Alz. You may find reading this to be helpful. You may be beyond the need for this information. This website has some wonderful information that you may find helpful.

Remember you are not alone. Every day I meet someone new caring for someone with Alz. Everyone is in a different place, yet there are many commonalities among these wonderful caregivers. They have heart, compassion and unfortunately a great deal of stress and at times guilt. The road a caregiver travels can be bumpy to say the least. Take a few minutes today to say a prayer for yourself, remember that you are doing the best that you can do, and most importantly do not take anything personally. This last was very difficult for me to remember during my journey. Today I am thankful for the times that I took a huge breath, a short walk, a moment on the deck to have a conversation with myself... Susan, this is not your mom speaking...this is not about you...this is a disease.

Hugs, my friends, your loved one... loves you. Take a moment to remember... a beautiful moment in time that you have shared with your loved one. That is the person you are caring for...that beautiful memory, moment/s...the person who inspired you to be the care giver you are today.

Robin, Margo and I are here if you need anything. Have a good day.

Susan

Good morning dear Care Givers,

In my note last week I asked all of you to come prepared to listen for His whisper…or if necessary shout. I sure did hear a lot of whispers and a few loud shouts, so I thought I would share some of what I heard. Please feel free to add to this and send to the group if you heard other whispers or shouts.

The first loud shout was THANK YOU for being so loving, caring and wonderful for coming today to share and to support each other. You are AWESOME!

Next, I heard the sweet whispers of praise for all that you are doing, that you are loved and supported and that God is with you at all times and all places. Some of you may not have heard this, but I heard clearly that He sometimes needs us to sit still for a few moments and just listen, breathe and listen, pray and listen.

I also heard Him whisper…YOU ARE NOT ALONE! People and resources are available. This group has names and numbers and much love and support to be shared. Do NOT hesitate to reach out to anyone of us, it makes us feel so blessed to be able to give back in our own loved ones' memories.

Finally, this was a whisper in my ear. I have a dear friend. But during the time with my mother I had to stop my relationship with her. She was too strong for me and sometimes her words were insensitive. I was in a delicate state, I felt if I had one blade of grass placed on my shoulder I would break and I was afraid my friend was that blade of grass. So I stopped all activities that involved her…it was difficult and I felt sad, but I know it was I needed to do. Two years after mom died, I am reconnected with her. I am stronger now. I am able to participate in our group activities once again. I know when to excuse myself from a conversation, to walk away. I heard this whisper because we all have to protect ourselves during this stressful time and surround ourselves with love, peace and calm, beauty and joy so that we have strength to deal with the stress that comes with the disease. Letting go does not have to be out of anger, it does not have to be forever, it can be for love of self and for your loved one, it can be for a short time or for as long as needed. There is no guilt or shame in this, it is what is. Remember whatever decisions you make at this time are the best decisions you know how to make.

So my dear friends, you need sleep, you need rest, you need support. This is a difficult journey. Do whatever it takes so that you will have enough strength that you will be able to be there for the entire journey. Three years later I am still catching up, I still rest when I need it, cry when I need it and seek others when I need them. I talk to mother every single day. I still see butterflies every day. I finally realize I am not crazy, just recovering from total exhaustion, both physically and emotionally. ALZ takes such patience and love and kindness, it is exhausting to the caregiver. Take care of YOU!

Much Love,

Me

Good Morning my friends,

Here it is a new week and just two weeks until we meet again. I am hoping all is well with you.

This week there is much talk about faith and prayer on the media. They even showed scientific proof that prayer/meditation builds a stronger cortex.

So what does this mean to us? My first thought was that my mother was drawn back to the church in the middle of her Alzheimer's ...she sought out help to get her to church, took classes and attended mass every Sunday as long as she could. My second thought is that the journey of ALZ as difficult as it was, strengthened my own faith. And my final thought is that... prayer/meditation and spiritual music may have a calming impact on our loved ones. Perhaps a recording of a favorite prayer or song would be a wonderful tool to have on hand.

This Holy Week may be the very time to focus on the spiritual being of our loved ones. Perhaps you can even bring back a childhood memory of this beautiful season.

Hugs my friends, you and your loved ones will be in my thoughts and prayers.

Susan

Good Morning Ladies,

I hope you have had time to enjoy this beautiful weather, the birds chirping, jasmine blooming, spring in the air. I am so grateful for spring.

Every day I hear a new story, read another article, see another news broadcast about ALZ. That is good news. It is finally getting the attention it needs. They are finally talking about the impact it has on families. They are finding new medications, great links to what causes ALZ. However, with that being said...it really does not change anything for you today...EXCEPT, you can be confident you are not alone and the behaviors of your loved one are not unique to you.

I just heard a story last week about one household where the grandchildren are now hating their grandmother, that saddened me so. While it is so difficult to explain to children, it is an opportunity to educate our children about this disease.

Take a moment today to remember the things you love about your loved one, write them down, post them if necessary but that is the person you are caring for, the one you love, that now has an incurable, inoperable disease. As all terminal illnesses, it brings pain. May you bear the pain and see your loved one for who they are. As they say...getting old is not for sissies. 😉

As always we look forward to seeing you and lending support to each other.

Hugs and have a beautiful week...don't forget to take care of the caregiver.

Susan

Happy Easter my Wonderful and Loving Care Givers!

Today is a day to rejoice and to celebrate. However you do it is up to you. I remember there was a time that I thought celebrations had to be a particular way, but during life's journey I realized that just is not true. Celebration is in your HEART and MIND!

So no matter what is planned for your day... make it a celebration, a celebration of life, of love and forgiveness. A celebration of YOU!

I am sitting here looking at a photo of my mother from her last Easter...it is one of my favorite keepsakes. We had just finished dinner and her oldest great-granddaughter came over to give her a hug. The look on her face is one of love and peace...that, my friends, is a celebration!

LOVE and PEACE. So take a moment on this Easter morning to hug someone you love, capture that feeling, that moment and cherish it, it is your golden ticket to LIFE, to a celebration.

How blessed are we to enjoy this Easter Morning...such a wonderful reminder of what was given up for us, so that we can live in the image and likeness of GOD. Let your light shine today, and every day, for we are so blessed to be loved. Be grateful for the celebration in your heart, for the love around you and for the peace that washes over you when you are hugged.

Let's make today's celebration full of Easter Hugs...hug everyone you see and just say Happy Easter, I love you! Wow!, now that is what I call a celebration of life.

Happy Easter my friends...this is the day of the GOLDEN EGG, when you find yours remember to cherish it...there are no two alike.

Love and many hugs my friends,

Me

GM My Amazing Care Givers,

Today is Sunday, a new day and a new week, and while we have been apart, it became a new month. Spring is in the air and we never know what to expect, from warm and blustery days to cool and calm sunrises, from rains and storms to gentle breezes and perfect skies.

This reminds me of the journey of caregiving.... "Life is like a box of chocolates; you never know what you are going to get." (Forrest Gump) So today I wish for you... blue skies, calm seas, gentle breezes, and a box of chocolates filled with nothing but your favorite candies! Won't that be a lovely day!

The wonder of what is next...in the ALZ journey...can cause the caregiver anxiety or stress. So, in thinking of the weather and the glory of spring, with all of its changes, do we wonder what the weather will bring? Do we worry or stress over tomorrow's predictions, or do we just take what comes and find the beauty of the day? So, let's just take it as it comes and not worry about tomorrow or later this afternoon...you never know what you will get...so just sit back, breathe, and watch it unfold. There is preparation we can do for stormy days, but we cannot make them disappear.

This reminds me of yesterday and my company. They woke up to gentle rains and a sky of clouds. They prepared for the weather, took showers, and made plans for a rainy day...and before the final shower was had, the sun was shining and the clouds moved out. Without a blink of the eye, the dad said... "Everyone in your bathing suits...it is beach time!" No stress, just the flow of the moment. It did not matter that we just showered for the day; we jumped into our suits and hit the shore! Wouldn't it be great if we could be like this with the ebb and flow of ALZ...just take it as it comes.

Now, I am the first to admit, this is easier said than done, but this is my wish for you: Take a breath and just go with the moment. Take it as it comes, prepare for the day, but when the weather changes, just enjoy what is happening. Whether the sun comes out or the clouds move in, find the beauty of that moment. "As I surrender my thoughts to love, God's power moves through me and I become a healer." (taken from my inspirational readings this morning.)

So, my wonderful caregivers, live in the moment. It is what we have. Prepare for the weather, but be ready to remove the jacket when the winds calm, the breezes slow, and the rains dry. And when the sun shines... remember... you did that... you made that sunshine because you took a breath and let it shine, shine, shine.

Thank you for caring, thank you for all the love you give every moment of every day! YOU are AMAZING!

Many hugs and much LOVE,

CARE GIVERS are amazing and loving people!

Me

To Susan...I cannot really express my gratitude to you, Robin, Margo and our support group for the help you gave Fred and me during the last year that my dear mom was with us.

It was a tough tough time, but thanks to our group, I was guided to help my mom in a very special way.

It was meeting with you and Gary, Susan, when my mom was having such a terrible time at the assisted living that helped so much.

You and Gary met us and discussed the problems of adjusting to a new place for my mama. You shared the times you had with your dear mom staying with you, and trying different places to care for her.

It made things REAL for me.

And then the day my mom passed, I called you, and we talked for at least an hour to help me through the first day, first week, first month, and year. Thank you for your weekly letters to guide me.

You have helped so many of us in many many ways..

God bless.

– Deanna and Fred Behmer

Good Afternoon my wonderful Friends and Care Givers:

I am so sorry I was unable to write yesterday, but I was flying home from a trip to Chicago with my four MI munchkins and when I arrived home I was exhausted...never got off the couch.

So, this exhaustion was a beautiful reminder...exhaustion is not ALL bad. Yes, I was tired, but tired from a beautiful experience. My exhaustion was physically draining, but the love and joy in my heart was overflowing. So, while I remember all too well the exhaustion of being a caretaker, I am asking you to take time this week, during the midst of that feeling, to see what you are feeling in your heart as well as in your physical being. I am confident you will find the joy and peace and love that this journey is bringing you.

I guess that thought brings me to all of our life journeys. It is all very simple and comes down to one thing: GRATITUDE!

"Gratitude is not only the GREATEST of virtues, but the PARENT of all others." – Cicero 106-43 BC. (So grateful my wonderful husband jotted this quote down for me.)

Here are just a few simple thoughts connected to GRATITUDE. Today I met with my Dr.'s Assistant. At first this made me very anxious, but it turns out, I benefited from this meeting. Martin is a cancer survivor and he was able to share some of the blessings that came from his journey, reminding me to be open to the power of gratitude for each journey we take along our life walk. For Martin, he believes he is much more able to connect to his patients, and I saw this today. His compassion was amazing and I was very grateful for this compassion and understanding. In sharing the emotions I was experiencing, he was able to say... "Yep...normal." So awesome to hear. So yes, when you are feeling overwhelmed or tired or frustrated or sad...NORMAL...just take a moment and BREATHE and do something for yourself. ☺

Mondays are no longer on my list of favorite days... I actually hope to wake up and find out it is Tuesday. But it never happens; Mondays continue to come. So, we were up at 5:00, off to Jax at 6:00, blood at 7:20, Dr. at 8:30 and chemo at 9:45. Yuck! But in truth it has been a lovely day. A dear friend came to hold my hand and share healing mantras for my listening pleasure. When I discovered I was not in a private room, in a chair rather than a cuddly bed, it was Anita who found out how to recline my chair, not the nurse. She was determined to make me as comfortable as possible. This was that little blessing I so needed, that whisper from God Himself, an angel at my side.

Please make sure you notice your daily dose of GOD and Angels, we sometimes just forget to realize that it is not a coincidence...but a MESSAGE...so GRATEFUL.... EXHAUSTED... but GRATEFUL!

Then when we finally made it home...I took my girls out...just in time to discover four beautiful hibiscuses on our bush and two lovely butterflies floating through our garden...oh so grateful to have a visit from above...I was so exhausted, but that made my heart full of peace and love and joy...so GRATEFUL.

So my friends, take that exhaustion and let the GRATITUDE follow. Notice those little things that can make your heart sing. Please do not take for granted any of your angels, any simple whisper from above. They are there for you, to ease your exhaustion so that you can see the glory of the journey..

Many hugs my sweet friends, this is a new day, be GRATEFUL, it is here for YOU! You are an ANGEL for your loved one...enjoy the ANGELS there for YOU!

Me

Good Morning My Sweet and Caring Friends,

Happy Sunday! The full moon is out my backdoor (or almost full) and the most gentle sunrise out my front window. So grateful to be up and enjoying these two simple miracles.

This morning the word DECISIONS has popped into my head. Think about all of the instantaneous decisions you make each and every day... Should I get up, what to wear, what to have for breakfast, cream or no cream, church or no church...on and on they go. We do not even realize that we are making these split-second decisions, but we are. We do not question ourselves about our decisions; we just move right into our decision with basically no thought at all. We ASSUME the decision is the correct decision for that moment.

So, I wonder then, why do we question ourselves, even doubt ourselves, when we are making those thought-provoking decisions? Every day you are making decisions for your loved ones, and there are times when you doubt yourself.

Today I want you to just make the decisions without question. Make it with the same confidence you make those instantaneous decisions. You know you are making them with God's guidance. You pray daily and that is why you are able to make those instantaneous decisions.

Guess what? He has you...for every decision. So please do not question or deliberate. KNOW you are doing the best that you can and that your decision is guided and strong. It is the correct decision for this moment. That does not mean it will not change later...but for now it is CORRECT...perhaps very difficult...but CORRECT!

You are a pillar of strength and love. You are wise beyond your years! Rejoice in your wisdom in decision-making. This week, do not question yourself. Just relax in the beauty of your knowledge and understanding of the situation. When someone sets an obstacle in your path...just know that you have the wisdom to avoid the obstacle and move forward.

DECISIONS...you've got this! They are CORRECT...they are what you KNOW! So instead of worrying or wondering, use those extra moments to just BREATHE! Because you are the DECISION-making QUEEN for the week. No doubts, no fears, just forward...avoiding all obstacles in your path.

Have a smooth sailing kind of week...free from worry or doubt...but sailing in the breezes of power and breath.

Enjoy this worry-free week, my friends. You GOT THIS! Many hugs, miss you all,

Me

HAPPY MOTHER'S DAY EVERYONE!

Today is your day! To borrow from The Hammock Community Church signage...How do you spell LOVE... MOTHER! That is just so true! There is nothing greater than a MOTHER's love...whether you are giving or receiving. So today we celebrate YOU! It is no wonder that many of our caregivers are female...it is that motherly love that drives us to care for those we love. It is that motherly love that opens up our hearts to others.

For some of us, we will begin by saying a little prayer to our mothers. For others, you will hold your mother's hand, and for yet others it will just be a phone call or a card in the mail or a simple thought about your mom. Whatever your situation with your mother...celebrate what she taught you, because no matter what it is you learned from her...you have or will pass it forward in some way.

A MOTHER'S love is much like your love for the loved one you are caring for or have cared for...unconditional. Notice UNCONDITIONAL does not have "PERFECT" in the middle. Moms make mistakes; they are far from perfect; but they are the best they know how to be at that moment in time. There is no rule book, there is no right and wrong way to mother, there just is MOTHER or MOM!

Some of the very best mothers I know do not have children of their own...yet they give unconditionally to others. Some of the best mothers I know made difficult choices, causing them great pain, but yet... they gave of themselves unconditionally. Mothers come in all sizes and shapes; they take many different forms; their love looks very different; yet they are LOVE.

Perhaps I will take editing privileges with the HCC signage...How do you spell MOTHER...CAREGIVER! Thank you from the bottom of my heart for being the CAREGIVER you are. You all look different, your journey is different, your LOVE is different, but yet you give unconditionally! It is not PERFECT, but it is the best you know at the moment!

Thank you for being the BEST MOTHER you know how to be at this moment in time...pass that unconditional LOVE forward to your children and grandchildren, for they will be the CAREGIVERS of the future...our CAREGIVERS.

Today, I am so GRATEFUL for all the MOTHERS in my life...there are many...some are younger, some are my age, some are older, but they are all loving and caring and wise and compassionate and beautiful, both inside and out. Today...I am GRATEFUL for my MOTHER...I still miss her every day...and feel her strength during my own journey.

Hugs dear friends...HAPPY MOTHER'S DAY...YOU deserve this day to celebrate YOU!

Me

GM My Sweet and Loving Caregivers,

Today is Sunday a new day and a new week...a time to look at PERSPECTIVE... "subjective evaluation of relative significance; a point of view...a mental view or outlook."

Our PERSPECTIVE is based upon our life experiences and what we are experiencing at this moment in time. It can and does change. Because contrary to some popular opinions... our PERSPECTIVE is not a fact, but, as the dictionary states, a "point of view"; a "mental outlook."

I am sure you are all thinking right about now....Susan has lost it... what does this have to do with us as caregivers? Well, it came to me this week that my PERSPECTIVE as caregiver has changed multiple times over the past five years.

In the beginning, my point of view was based solely on my being the caregiver and what I saw was through the eyes of the caregiver...myself. It was a pretty one-sided point of view, for sure. I often wondered why others did not help, or why they could not see how exhausted I was, or why they could not give or do more, or why my mother was not the number one priority on everyone's minds.

As time went on, I met other caregivers and I could hear their perspective and see another side of the caregiving journey. I saw it was not all about me and my mother; there were others who had needs and who were giving of themselves and doing it selflessly. There were greater and different challenges that were being met selflessly and without doubt or question. My PERSPECTIVE changed. I saw caregiving from the eyes and hearts of others, and it opened so many doors and I discovered there was strength to be gained from hearing different PERSPECTIVES.

And now my friends, my PERSPECTIVE is from an entirely different place...it is coming from the other side, and that is what I want to share today. Being the caregiver to a loved one with ALZ or Dementia is probably one of the most challenging caregiving journeys, because they cannot always express what they feel. So hopefully today, I will be able to help you see just a small piece of their PERSPECTIVE...just a small view through their eyes.

The first thing is WONDER ...How did I get here? This is not how it was supposed to be... I am the CAREGIVER... I am here to take care of your needs. This is my job. And then comes WORRY: Are you OKAY, how are you doing, how can I help, what can I do for you, and yet, in the end you just keep caring for me. Everything about this feels wrong. I can't seem to understand what has happened. My PERSPECTIVE has been blindsided.

And then finally, we realize, there is nothing we can do, and...GRATITUDE kicks in. So much gratitude and really no way to ever thank you for all of the tender care, the kindness you show every day, the love you are able to give so unconditionally, and all I can do is receive it. So... sometimes I smile when you enter the room, sometimes I am still so you think I am asleep or do not need anything at all, sometimes I just hold your hand so you can rest, and sometimes I just simply pray that you will be taken care of, that you will know how grateful I am for all that you are doing.

That, my friend, is just a glimpse of the PERSPECTIVE from the other side... GRATITUDE! So grateful for all that you do, for the kind words, the text, the e-mails, for the cards, the prayers, the little things you never thought you would have to do but are doing, the love, the unconditional love that you show every day.

We may not always be able to show it or say it, but I promise you...your loved one's heart is filled with GRATITUDE...even during those moments it feels as if they do not appreciate you at all...they are GRATEFUL. So please hold this PERSPECTIVE in your heart as you wander the path of caregiver...you are their life line and they/we are GRATEFUL for all you are doing...there is no way to ever THANK YOU enough...I promise.

Enjoy this new day, take another look out the window of life and you will see the sparkle in their eye...it is GRATITUDE for YOU and all YOU do!

Many hugs my friends and much love,

Me

GM My wonderful CareGivers,

Today I choose the word CELEBRATE to share with you. Today Gary and I celebrate our fortieth anniversary. And as we celebrate this milestone I would like you to CELEBRATE your life journey with your loved ones. We have spent a few days looking through old photo albums and reminiscing; it has been a fun way to remember all of the good times and the sad times of our life together. We were such babies at the time, we had both forgotten how we looked forty years ago today. 😊

But I feel confident if you take time to look back at some old photos...you will begin to see your loved one start to REMEMBER many of the pieces of their life journey. They will most likely remember their young self more than they remember who they see in the mirror today.

So let's all use today to CELEBRATE life, love, and each other! After all, this is just a day we chose forty years ago...it could have been any day of the year...that is what is so wonderful about life celebrations...they can happen anytime and I firmly believe we need to have more celebrations in our lives!

Please celebrate with us today, don't wait, as we do not know what tomorrow will bring. Give that extra hug, take time to look back, walk down memory lane, get out that extra special china, jump for joy, smile for no reason, today is a new day and you deserve to CELEBRATE it as much as we do.

Love you all so much and miss seeing and hugging each one of you.

Take care of you...the Care Taker.

Me

GM My Beautiful Care Givers:

Happy Memorial Day weekend! Happy official beginning of Summer! Happy Sunday! Happy last Sunday in this month! Happy Day! In just two weeks you will all be together to celebrate the day! Yahoo...meantime...let's use this Memorial Day weekend to REMEMBER.

Let's take today and tomorrow to REMEMBER the good times, the loving times, the BEST of times. So, I am changing things up just a bit for this week. What I would like to ask each one of you to do is to write one beautiful memory you have of your loved one...it can be from yesterday or from the first day you met. It can be humorous or beautiful...any memory you would like to share about your loved one.

I will begin. I have so many wonderful memories of my mother and I love each and every one of them when they pop up out of nowhere and make me smile. But this one Gary & I both cherish for many reasons. It is humorous and every time we go to the Turtle Shack we cannot help but think of my mother.

It was a Sunday and we always went to 9:00 mass with mom. She loved the coconut shrimp at the Turtle Shack, so after mass we would call in an order so we could take it home for her lunch; she thought it was too early to stop and eat. This particular Sunday we went to the later mass so we decided to stop at the TS for lunch. While mom loved the coconut shrimp, I also knew that she loved a good burger and that deciding was difficult for her at this point in time. So I said to Gary...I will order a burger and we can order coconut shrimp for mom...that way I can trade with her if she would prefer a burger. So that is what we did. Everything came out and we began eating. I noticed my mother eyeing...not my burger but Gary's. So I asked her if she would like a taste of the burger and she said yes. Gary quickly cut her a two-bite triangle piece of his burger for her to sample. She ate it right down and then quickly went back to eating her shrimp...so I thought OK...she just wanted a taste.

As we were walking to the car I asked my mother if she liked the shrimp and she said...Yes, but that was the smallest burger I have ever seen! I felt absolutely horrible that I had not offered her more burger, but we laugh to this day that mother thinks the TS has the smallest burgers in town! She always wanted the CS after that...because their burgers were too small!

I think this is such a great example of how the minds of an ALZ/Dementia person are operating and we have no clue and the THINGS they do remember can be quite funny!

Please share a MEMORY this week. It does not have to be from the journey; it can be any memory new or old...my mom and I were best of friends, I am so GRATEFUL for her love and I think about her every day with Gratitude, Love and Affection.

Have a wonderful weekend walking down MEMORY lane my friends,

Hugs and much love,

Me

GM My Care Giving Friends,

Today is the first Sunday of June and we have definitely made it to summer. I hope all of you had a great week.

I have talked with several caregivers this week, including my own special guy, and every time I am truly amazed by your unconditional love and care. My conversations and thoughts have continued to move toward two prayers that I said over and over during my journey with mom and now daily.

The first a friend sent, I still have it posted. *"God our father, walk through my house and take away all of my worries and illness and please watch over and heal my family."* I love this simple request, a prayer for every day.

The second was the Serenity Prayer. A friend sent it to me yesterday, not knowing how often I say this prayer. We all know it. It is a powerful prayer.

"God grant me the Serenity to ACCEPT the things I cannot change.

The COURAGE to change the things I can
and the WISDOM to know the difference."

Two simple prayers with so much meaning. Today I say these prayers for all of us. The power of prayer is incredible, the miracles that follow are amazing, the strength we are given...healing.

There are days we will cry, to cleanse our minds, hearts and souls. There are days we feel weak and tired, the prayer will guide us back to our inner strength. There are days we feel alone and then we remember, we are NEVER ALONE.

So my dear friends, two simple prayers, with the power to carry us forward. Miracles happen. We live here in paradise, where we have each other and a beautiful world around us to remind us that GOD is here, with us.. ALL the WAY...EVERY DAY!

May these two prayers bring you peace this week, may you see the beauty in this new day, this new week. Breathe, then pray, then breathe again. You are LOVED!

Hugs,

Me

Good Morning Caregivers,

I hope all of you have had a wonderful week. I want to begin by saying THANK YOU for all that you do each and every day. For all of the little things that go unnoticed but that I know you do...the phone calls, the hugs, the preparing, the patience, the tender moments, the struggles, the calm, the breath that gets you through the moment. Hugs, you deserve them.

This week take a moment each day to think about, even write down, one thing that you are grateful for about the loved one you are caring for, during this difficult time. It is funny, but during cancer, or any other illness that is so easy, so a part of the journey, but with ALZ, we sometimes have to remind ourselves about why we are caring for this person. I remember during my most difficult days with my mom, someone said, "Was your mom always difficult?" My first response was to say yes...but after a long walk, breathing and looking back, I remembered the wonderful mother she was. I remembered my best friend, who would never do anything to hurt me, who was always my support. I am so grateful for my mother and sorry for her disease that interrupted our beautiful relationship for a while when I was blinded by the illness. Remember to take the blindfolds off every day and see the person.

72

Today be grateful for the person you love and are caring for. The disease is not lovely, but the person is still your loved one.

Remember to care for the caregiver every day, a smile, a hug, a bouquet of flowers, a song on the radio, a walk on the sand, whatever YOU need take care of you.

Hugs and have a great week,

Me

Good Morning you wonderful caregivers:

I love Sundays because it is not only a new day but the beginning of a new week. I like to think of it as a chance to start fresh, which is really truly every moment of each day, but Sunday is a restart for an entire week...I just love that.

So with that being said, I would like to encourage you to use today to begin a GRATITUDE journey. It is not very difficult and I have found it to be a wonderful and beautiful journey. This is all you need to do. Each morning when you first get out of bed...take one moment to write down, state out loud, tell your loved one, or e-mail me ...one thing you are grateful for this very moment...anything at all...and then one thing you are grateful for that includes your loved one that you are caring for.

So, today I am grateful for this group, you are amazing ladies and I am so grateful that the journey with my mom's ALZ brought you into my life.

Have a wonderful week and a day filled with the gratitude's of life's simple pleasures.

Hugs and remember to take a few moments to care for yourself.

Me

Good Morning to the Caregivers of the Year!

Here it is a new day, a new week and the end of a month! Wow! Where does the time go?

I just saw in the newspaper that CNN will show a documentary on the journey of Glen Campbell and ALZ. I will be watching. It may be too difficult for those of you in the middle of the journey or who have just ended the journey to watch tonight, but you may want to record it for later. I will be watching and will be glad to share any wonderful tips or news that comes from the program.

While I am so glad that the famous have brought attention to this disease, and that Glen Campbell's journey will be documented, I am really more PROUD that we are documenting our own loved ones journey each month. By getting together and sharing and helping each other, we are each documenting our loved one's story. Thank you!

More good news: Yesterday someone came up to me and said, "I have heard there is a wonderful support group for ALZ in the Hammock!" It is us! It made my heart soar. So, I am here to say THANK YOU, I am so GRATEFUL that each of you has been willing to take the risk of coming and sharing your story, to make a "documentary" of the journey of your loved one with each other. Our loved ones deserve this and YOU deserve this time together. We are a team of loving and caring people who will make a difference in the lives of our loved ones. Thank you for caring, thank you for sharing, thank you for being the wonderful care giver you are.

Remember to take a moment each morning to be grateful for something, to give yourself a hug, a smile, a little love and rest. You are a wonderful caregiver, and your compassion is not only helping your loved one but so many others.

Thank you for all you do...it is so appreciated!

Hugs to all and may you see a simple miracle each day this week.

Susan

GM My Beautiful Friends,

I am so sorry to have missed sending you a weekly message yesterday, but getting home took all the energy I could muster. Hopefully you will all be meeting shortly to support one another through this journey.

During my six-day stay in the hospital I met so many wonderful, caring and loving caregivers. From Dr.'s. to PA's, to nurses, to technicians, to cleaning crew, they all gave a piece of themselves to every patient. A warm smile, a hug, a caring word, a thumb's up, to medication, advice, you name it, I got it. It was all lovely.

But I also had a great deal of time to think about your role and I realized I have given you the wrong title...so I will no longer refer to you as the caregivers, or care takers...you are much more...you are your loved ones' true ADVOCATE.

There is a huge difference between these two roles. While both take heart, kindness, gentleness, support and love, a care taker/giver does not know the heart and soul of the patient like you, the ADVOCATE, does.

It took being the patient and being so grateful that I had Gary, my wonderful advocate, there to support ME, the person he knows and loves. I appreciate and am grateful for all the enthusiasm and kindness, the love and patience of each of the caregivers, but I am truly grateful that I had an ADVOCATE, not helping me with every little need, but making sure my real needs were met. That is the difference, my friends, you the ADVOCATE see the big picture, you KNOW, really KNOW what is best for your loved one. Do not doubt yourself, let others be the caregivers, be it family members or paid caregivers, let them help under your guidance, but NO... is an acceptable answer. ☺

I needed help through the night, Gary needed some sleep during the night, so the caregivers were my angels, but during the day and when it came to medications, decisions were not made unless my ADVOCATE was awake and listening...Gary would simply say...need me hon...and I could answer no, just going to the bathroom, or yes, we need to make a medical decision.

Please, my dear friends, remember, you cannot do everything, be the wonderful ADVOCATE you are and when you need a caregiver, let them be your support team. After all, you are the one who knows the heart and soul of your loved ones, and they need a well-rested, thoughtful, caring and loving ADVOCATE... YOU! Take care of you, so that you can take care of your loved one.

Have a wonderful week my wonderful ADVOCATES! Take care of you so you can ADVOCATE for your loved one. The journey is long and difficult, they need you...healthy and happy. Let others assist, with your guidance, give the caregivers directions, so you can rest and make it very clear that your directions are to be followed. ☺

Love and miss all of you so much.

Many hugs and much love,

Me

P.S. I started this at 6:30 and it is now 9:00...slow and steady wins the race. My ADVOCATE made sure I rested. ☺

Dear Susan,

"A woman is like a tea bag...you never know how strong she is until she gets in hot water," said Eleanor Roosevelt. You, my friend are VERY strong!! You have been an inspiration to me since I first met you. Thank you so much for all your work, your words, and your wisdom. You have helped me through a very difficult time in my life in dealing with my mother, and helping my husband in understanding and caring for his younger brother. Many, many thanks.
– Nina Ellison

GM My Wonderful Advocates,

Happy Father's Day to all of your loved DADS, be it father, husband or son! May today be a restful day for all of them.

Tomorrow is the official start of SUMMER, a new season, a season filled with laughter and outdoor activities, vacations and late night memories. 😊 While here in FL it is both hot and humid, it is also a great time to just relax and CHILL...the perfect reminders for ADVOCATES!

What better time to sit out at the ocean shore, a luxury we enjoy by living here, sip an ice cold lemonade or beverage of your choice and reminisce of summers past. Perhaps an outing is too much for your loved one, how about bringing in photos of summer vacations to share with them.

There is a wonderful children's book titled "Wilfrid Gordon McDonald Partridge" by Mem Fox. It is the story of a young boy who lives next to an assisted living home and he has a favorite friend there who is losing her memory. Wilfrid asks all his friends at the AL home what a memory is and they each give him a definition...he promptly goes home and fills a basket of items that fit their definition...things from long ago, that make you laugh, etc. He brings the basket and items to his dear friend and shares them one at a time until they are both laughing and enjoying the day and....REMEMBERING!

That, my dear friends, is the story of summer, the story of memories. Take time during these "lazy, hazy, crazy days of summer" to REMEMBER. Remember the things that make you laugh, feel warm all over, something from long ago. For every Season there is a REASON...enjoy these dog days of summer...just REMEMBER.

Much love my friends, take time for you, just sit and relax and chill.. too hot for much of anything else. 😊

Hugs,

Me

P.S. Speaking of children's books, when Mother was no longer able to read her novels, she still enjoyed picking up children's books, and if nothing more, she enjoyed the pictures and telling the story.

P.P.S. One of the greatest memories of my DAD, who died when I was just fourteen, is that he taught me how to pick a great husband and advocate! I am so blessed. I am confident your spouse would say the very same thing about YOU!

GM Sweet Advocates,

Today is the last Sunday in June, and the warm, muggy days of summer are upon us. Just the weather alone can make us feel fatigued, especially if we try to do too much. Fatigue can make us feel tired and cranky and even sick, so this is the time you must really take care of both you and your loved one. What may seem like a simple outing, a common everyday practice, could be much more rigorous than just last month. So be careful and plan well for the heat, with short outside time and plenty of fluids to drink, for both you and your loved one.

I realized this morning that in the past I have drawn my writing from you, from your strength, from your concerns, from your love and experiences, and now I am not able to draw on those beautiful conversations and the words do not flow as easily. However, last week a friend sent me a booklet entitled "Christian at Ease." It is about the promises of God during adversity and prosperity. She found it helpful during her life struggles, and so have I found it a lovely read during my own battle with cancer.

I cannot share the booklet with you but just give you a gentle reminder that God is with you all the way, not just when things are going well, but during your worst and most difficult hours He has promised to be there with you and see you through.

There are times our hearts are so heavy, as during the Orlando crisis, that we may wonder what or why, two questions I try to avoid. The only answer to these questions should they arise is prayer, so my friends today I just remind you to meditate on the positive, breathe through the stress and know you are loved and prayed for daily. I know that will make you smile...just to know you are loved and that others are with you all the way to the finish line.

I remember praying to let my mother be at peace, I remember feeling guilty at times for that prayer, but there is no guilt, as it was a prayer for her peace and today I understand it more fully than ever before. So, my dear friends, today I pray for you and your loved ones. May you draw strength in knowing God is with you all the way and we are here for you should you need anything. While I cannot physically help you, I can pray for whatever need you may have at the time. Meanwhile, I will keep it generic. Dear God, please bless these wonderful advocates and give them the strength and love they need for this difficult journey.

Much love my friends, stay cool and hydrated, cranky is the last thing we need. ☺

Me

Happy 4th of July weekend to my Fabulous Advocates!

INDEPENDENCE is a great word to think about today. Here it is the 4th of July weekend, our own Independence Day, celebrated with fireworks, cookouts, and fun with family and friends. We love the 4th of July, our greatest summer celebration!

Our loved ones also love their independence, and the fear of losing this can cause anxiety and paranoia. Any feeling of independence that we can give them will help to calm these fears. While they cannot drive, perhaps they can go for a ride in their car. While they can no longer live alone, perhaps they can visit for a while. Unfortunately, eventually, they will lose or have lost their independence, and rides and visits will no longer be an option. When this happens then we, their advocates, need even greater patience! Yes, it will take more love, more patience and more strength to help them through their loss. And along with this...it takes more of our TIME as they become more and more dependent on us or others.

Today take a moment to think about how much we all love our Independence and all of the great battles that have been and are fought to secure our Independence. When we look at it through our own passion for Independence, we will have a greater understanding of the feelings of loss our loved ones must be dealing with on a daily basis. What a struggle for them.

So today, be patient, be empathetic, be loving... Independence is a RIGHT we have fought for, celebrated, and enjoyed for our entire lives...the loss is unbearable. If they can handle the fireworks, let them, but if nothing else take them to a celebration of Independence Day that they can appreciate, with songs and flags, things they know and love.

I will never forget going to the first 4th of July celebration at the Windsor. All of these wonderfully patriotic WWII survivors all gathered around to celebrate. My friend and I sat there with mom and we could not recognize any of the songs...no "Yankee Doodle Dandy," no "God Bless America," no flags waving, no God Bless the USA, no "America the Beautiful," no marching, no patriotism. This was something all of these wonderful folks would be able to appreciate, Independence Day. I cried for all of us. I was truly angry. The following year, mom was no longer at the Windsor, but I made sure everyone had flags, and decorations for hats and wheelchairs...while I cannot sing...I can march and I can say a word or two that will get these wonderful patriotic friends ready to celebrate...Independence Day.

So, whatever it takes to give them a little feel of Independence Day...tomorrow is the day to share it. Get out that red, white and blue, wave those flags with pride and sing those songs that make your heart soar...they will REMEMBER and they will FEEL and that is your gift for this Independence Day!

Happy 4th of July my friends. Happy Independence Day! Just take a moment or two to REMEMBER...what a luxury...so GRATEFUL for the memories.

Hugs and much love,

Me

GM Fabulous Advocates,

I have done several readings this week and the majority of them involved LOVE. So that is my word for today...LOVE. After the past two weeks, I can think of no better reminder for all of us.

So, LOVE is our thought for the week and for me that means...UNCONDITIONAL LOVE. What a powerful tool that is, when we are LOVED or when we LOVE UNCONDITIONALLY. I remember all too well that there were times during my mom's journey with ALZ that I began to doubt her unconditional love, and it was so very painful, just the doubt that slipped in and stole that love from me. But as I became a stronger advocate and had a better understanding of the disease, I realized it was not my mom but the disease that was making me doubt her love.

This morning is our reminder that we are always and forever loved unconditionally; do not allow anything or anyone to take that away from you, not even for a moment. Unconditional love is why you are the wonderful advocate that you are. Walking through ALZ/Dementia with a loved one is not for those who cannot love unconditionally. Perhaps, that is why, at times, we see our paid caregivers falter. They do not see our loved ones the same way we do, they do not have the feeling of unconditional love from our loved ones. The caregivers that have that special touch...they understand unconditional love.

So this morning my wonderful friends, remember you are loved, when words or actions speak differently, have no fear, you are loved. God is there, He will carry you through. As you feel the love, share the love, it is the only way to make it through the difficult times.

Tomorrow when you get together, give each other an extra warm hug, an unconditional love hug, from the depths of your heart. Someone in that room needs it more than you know. Go ahead and give them one from me as well, for that hug and that love is what will carry us through the difficult times.

Hugs my friends and much unconditional love for you,

Me

Good Morning Ladies,

I just wanted to take a moment to thank all of you for coming to share, hug and listen to each other.

After each of our gatherings it takes me a few hours to collect my emotions because the journey is so different for each of us, yet so similar because of the nature of the disease. I often worry that I am frightening those who are newer to this disease, as my mother was extremely difficult and it was very painful for me. My mother had been my best friend since my dad died when I was fourteen. We talked daily. To hear the things she said and to watch the disease progress broke my heart. As I have shared many times, I often felt alone as I did not want to burden my husband with more than he was already doing. I often felt I was on the verge of a nervous breakdown. Long walks and prayerful meditation every opportunity I was given... was truly the only way I was able to remind myself that it was a DISEASE and not my mother and that

89

I was doing the BEST that I knew how. Those words live loud and strong in my heart and they are words I will be ever grateful for...it is the DISEASE and I did the BEST I knew how!

I have shared this because that is what we are doing in our group...the BEST we know how. WE are not experts, we are a group who are sharing opinions...whatever you decide will be the CORRECT decision for you and it will be the BEST decision you can make. So when you make a difficult decision...have no REGRETS and move forward knowing you made the decision with love and the best information you have at that moment. If you need someone to listen, we are here, if you need a blessing to move forward, we give it, whatever you need we are here and I am confident, having met with each of you, that your decision is based on much prayer and love and will be made with great guidance.

Margo brought the Parade magazine from June 21, it is true, you are not alone. Did you know ALZ is the 6th leading cause of death in the US and it is the only cause in the top 10 that can't be prevented, cured or slowed down? 5.3 percent of Americans of all ages already have the disease. Every 67 seconds someone in the US develops the disease. You are making a difference, your care and your love and your willingness to share is making a difference and together we will make a difference, not only for our loved ones but for so many others.

Thank you for caring, thank you for sharing, thank you for being willing to take the caregiver journey; it is not for lightweights. Your faith, your love, your compassion make you the strong women that you are and I am so grateful that you are a part of my life journey and please remember...had my mother not had ALZ...I would most likely not have met you. I am so grateful for that journey, it has truly been life-altering for me. While difficult, I am so grateful, I have such a strong connection to my mom and so much more because of ALZ.

Hugs my friends, thank you for all you do,

Susan

GM To the Shining Stars of the Universe,

While I hope you had a wonderful week, whatever happened is over and today is a new day, a new week. Enjoy the wonderful memories and let go of anything that is not fun to keep. This is a new week, a time to enjoy the simple miracles of life that we sometimes miss because life is so busy.

So this week my thought is...SLOW and EASY. Yes, just take it slow and easy and enjoy the simple little things life brings. Have you ever noticed that sometimes God just slows us down, I think it is His way of whispering..."have you noticed?"

My husband is really good at this, and it was so important during my mother's journey with ALZ. At times when I was hurrying to get the tasks of the day done, Gary would notice the turtle outside eating grass and bring mother out to enjoy that simple pleasure, or the bird nest in the mailbox across the street. I would have missed that and so would my mother, had it not been for Gary's SLOW and EASY manner in enjoying life. The truth is, even though we might have spent 30 minutes just sitting and watching these simple life treasures, everything got done, and in fact I felt more at peace getting them done, because I had paused to BREATHE and enjoy life.

While we have always enjoyed "deck time," during my mother's journey and now my own journey with cancer, "deck time" is definitely one of the greatest pleasures of my day. We wait until the warm afternoon breezes are just perfect, sit out, prop our feet up and just talk and reminisce. I have several wonderful photos of mom sitting on the deck, with her sweet dog Bonnie, and we just chatted and chatted about memories. Now both Bonnie, and her sister Summer love deck time as well, and nothing gets done, except for enjoying life's simple treasures...MEMORIES! What could be more important, especially for someone in the midst of the ALZ/dementia journey, when memories are so difficult to find, than just sitting and remembering? 😊

So my friends, my thought is SLOW and EASY. Do not worry about what needs to be done. Be like Gary: see the moment and seize it, you have no idea what treasured memories those unplanned moments in time will bring. I know there are times that you are thinking...no way we could just sit and do nothing. But remember... that is what I thought for a long time, but in truth, those slow moments often brought an agitated mom to a peaceful place...SLOW and EASY. Your loved one feels the stress you are feeling. What my mom and I felt/feel with Gary is PEACE...no hurries...no worries. I thank God every day that He gave me this man who is my constant reminder that all will be well....just breathe.

I am headed to pick hibiscus, light a candle, enjoy the music playing, put my feet up and just BE. What will you do today to enjoy life's simple pleasures...to help your loved ones relax and breathe and remember? I hope you will take it SLOW and EASY and just make beautiful memories during some part of your otherwise hectic day.

Many hugs and much love my friends,

Me

P.S. So proud of Carolyn and Sandi for the difficult decisions they had to make and the beautiful outcomes. SLOW and EASY my friends, just BREATHE!

GM My Wonderful Advocates and Caregivers:

Yes, I have doubled your title, because I realized in retrospect, you are both, advocate and caregiver 😊 So why strip you of one title to embrace another? I should have just added advocate. Such is life: often change is an improvement, but change also needs to embrace the past in order for it to improve the now.

This morning my thought is MIRACLE. Everyone has a picture of Miracles in their head, I know I did, but just like your title, it has changed. I used to consider miracles to be big, beautiful, amazing...something to behold and to share with the world. That most likely I would see very few if any in my lifetime, but of course, I would read about them.

However, when my Gratitude Journey began a few years back, shortly after mom passed away, I began to see MIRACLES in a totally different light. My view changed, but as your title, it encompasses the past to make my picture a new and improved version of the old. I still believe in those huge miracles, the ones we read about, those life-changing miracles that we may never see in our lifetime, but I also realize and appreciate the daily, simple, sparkling miracles that we witness and sometimes ignore...or at least I did.

So this week, beginning today, I would like you to focus on the daily miracles in your life. I can promise that when you take time to notice them, they will definitely bring a smile to your face.

Let me share a few examples of daily miracles, what I now realize are the simple pleasures of life.

✧   As dry as it has been, we have had no rain for weeks, much is turning brown around us...yet every morning a hibiscus on my favorite hibiscus plant opens, just for me.

✧   Sandi was seeking a place for her mom, and her mom has a new refuge. ☺

✧   Carolyn was searching for the answer and the support group gave her the courage she needed to find that answer.

✧   Butterflies are a symbol of my mom. I see one daily, and I have received nine anonymous crocheted butterflies in the mail since I have been sick...no one has confessed to sending these, but each one arrives just when I need it most. ☺

✧   The sun shines on the Atlantic Ocean in such a beautiful way each morning that it makes my heart soar, no matter how tired I might be feeling.

✧   Though I have not seen you since March, I know you are still there and you are still meeting to support one another.

Though ALZ is a difficult disease, there is much love and joy that comes from being an advocate/caregiver, mostly from our own hearts, knowing that our loved ones are well taken care of because of our unconditional love for them.

This does not mean that I do not still pray for that huge miracle...for the CURE for ALZ, for the CURE for CANCER, but instead of waiting for that miracle we will one day read about, I am now able to enjoy small, simple miracles that keep my faith strong and my heart happy. Daily, simple miracles are the ones we sometimes miss, yet they are the real miracles of life, the life-changers. This journey would be too long if the only miracle I could see would be years down the road. I might be disappointed if the only miracle I could see was a CURE. I am grateful that every day when I open my eyes, I see the miracle of life, my husband by my side, friendships all around, my girls in my lap, the sunshine on the water, the birds singing, the strength to get out of bed, the beauty of this new day and the joy of the smile of my loved one.

So my friends, enjoy the miracles of this new day and week. Find your hibiscus and enjoy it. If you have the time, send me a note sharing the miracle of your day. I would love to hear about it.

Much love, Many hugs and the Joy of life's simple Miracles,

Me

GM My Care Giving Advocates,

Can you believe that today is the end of July and the beginning of a new day, a new week? That today turns the page on a month gone by only to open a new chapter, a new month...August! What a POWERFUL day, and POWER is my word for this week.

There are many times of every day and every month that I have a feeling of powerlessness, but when I take a moment to stop and breathe, to pray, I realize that I hold the POWER for what will be in this given moment. That I alone, with God's help, can make it a positive moment or a moment where I sense hopelessness. Realizing that it is my choice gives me the feeling of POWER!

During the journey of ALZ and now the journey of cancer, there were many nights that I went to bed exhausted and feeling that I might not be able to go on, that the task in front of me was too daunting, that others could not understand how difficult it was, that I was not that strong, my POWER was minimal. Then amazingly, I would waken in the morning refreshed by God's peace during the night and know that it was a new day, a new moment, that I did have the POWER to choose and that my choice was to make this the best day ever.

Sometimes, that choice was to give myself a much-needed break, to get my hair done and just laugh and enjoy, to walk and breath, or just BE. Sometimes my choice was to make my mother laugh out loud, to make sure she could remember some little thing that would make her smile (usually a great grandchild did that, or for that matter...any child). Sometimes it was something bigger, like having the nerve to ask Robin and Margo if they would start an ALZ support group with me and hearing them say yes! Wow, am I ever grateful for that day and all the POWER it has given to each one of us. Where did I get that nerve? We all know only too well that God that night replenished my soul, mind and body with the POWER to ask.

Big or small, it does not matter, the choices we make are what give us the POWER to make it a beautiful day, week, month. Today I am making two choices, one pretty simple, I am making word stones to take to my fellow cancer patients when I next return to the Mayo...simple little stones with a positive thought for them for that moment in time... Hope, Faith, Love, Joy, Breathe, Peace...what would your word be?

Secondly, a little bigger choice, the POWER of a letter to my friends asking for a donation to find a cure for ALZ. It is never easy to ask for donations, but ask I will and I will be EMPOWERED, by my choice to do my best to make a difference.

So what will you do today to EMPOWER yourself, to give you the much-needed strength that you need to make this a beautiful day, to close the door on July and open the window to August?

Today I would like to close with a quote from my daily readings..."My power in the world will emerge from the power in my heart." What does your heart hold today? "Whatever I do today, whatever effort large or small that I exert on behalf of healing the world, can be turned into a mighty work. I dedicate my efforts...my work both personal and professional...to be used by God. I will be amazed by what He then brings forth."

I cannot wait to see what your Powers bring forth, today, tomorrow and always.

Hugs my sweet friends, miss you much,

Me

Good Morning my Care Giving Advocates,

Happy first Sunday in August. I hope you had a POWERFUL week.

This week my thoughts are of GRATITUDE. There is so much that I am grateful for this morning: the good wishes of family and friends, the gentle rains that we had after a long dry spell, the sun that shines every morning, the life journey I have been blessed with, the love of my life, our girls, LIFE... so grateful.

Before my commitment to a 40-day Gratitude Journey that is now several years long, I often took some things for granted. Now each morning before I get involved in life's hectic journey, I take time to be GRATEFUL, grateful for the little things that can so easily be taken for granted.

This morning I am Grateful for YOU and the support you have given to each other, for your love and compassion for others, for the strength and power you hold, for your willingness to smile, to enjoy, to hug, to embrace. GRATITUDE has allowed me to be grateful for both the ups and downs of life. I am grateful for the ability to breathe when life gets tough, to understand that I am not alone, that God will help me through the most difficult journeys and that He has placed each and every one of you in my path for a reason.

So this morning, I am Grateful for YOU, for today, for breath, for life's journey... no matter what it brings, for the slow pace of cancer, ALZ, whatever it is that slows us down to take time to be GRATEFUL. I am GRATEFUL for each and every moment of Life!

Please take a moment and think about the things that make your life so special, the people, the love, the hearts and souls that have touched you along the way of life's journey. God placed each person/item there for YOU because You are so special. I am so GRATEFUL for YOU!

Hugs my friends, GRATITUDE will carry you through. It will allow you to say thank you every morning for life's simple joys and difficult roads...for the loved one who slowed you down and has given you time to smell the roses along the way...so GRATEFUL for those slow moments in time. For those who have gone before us and continue to hold our hand, be GRATEFUL, they gave us some of life's very best lessons. GRATITUDE each day will keep the blues away!

Much Love and Many Hugs,

Me

GM My Wonderful Care Giving Advocates,

It was absolutely wonderful to talk to some of you on Monday. I so look forward to being there to hug you in person, and that may very well be at our next meeting. Please keep those prayers coming.

This morning my word is LIFE and this is dedicated to Gary's and my dear friend Mandi, who needs our support very badly at this time in her LIFE. We all know those days, months, years, that nothing seems to go our way, that everything painful that can happen, happens. We can tell you the date it all began, but seldom remember when it finally ended. We have our own stories and have heard the stories of others. It makes us question our faith, get angry with GOD, doubt ourselves, feel alone, and even want to give up. Hence the words... "but for the grace of God."

So my dear friends, though we are all traveling our own rocky road and need prayers ourselves, this morning I ask you to send prayers up for Mandi. A prayer that she...feels His grace and can let go of the things she cannot change. That she feels the strength of our prayers and the love of others around her. That her aching heart feels compassion and love. That she understands that a decision to let others do does not mean she has failed. That she realizes she is not alone. That she understands that sometimes LIFE is just difficult, but that God is there and she will get through... "but for the grace of God."

And this my friends, this morning, is my prayer for Mandi and for YOU. But for the grace of God...may we may make it through this difficult time in our LIFE. May we feel a hug, let something go so that we can once again breathe, know we are not alone, understand that we have done everything we can do, and feel LOVE in our LIFE journey. That today we take the day to take care of ourselves, because today we need to deal with LIFE itself, to find the help and support that we need.

Thank you for your prayers for Mandi. Thank you for all you do. May each one of you feel the GRACE of God during your daily walk through LIFE.

Hugs and much love,

Me

GM My Wonderful Advocates/CareGivers,

Today the song, "You Are My Sunshine" comes to mind. While not all the words are appropriate for today, the verse is what is playing over and over in my sleepless head. 😊

You are my sunshine, my only sunshine

You make me happy when skies are gray

You'll never know dear, how much I love you

Please don't take my sunshine away.

I have always enjoyed this catchy little tune, I sing it to the grandkids when we walk to the beach. My mom used to sing it to us. They have singing flowers that sing this verse and today it reminds me of you. The line, "You'll never know dear, how much I love you" rings very true with ALZ patients. They can't tell you or show you at times, but when you take a moment to remember the way it was, and that this is a disease, then you will remember that they do.

While we desperately need rain and I pray for it each day, it is the sunshine that carries me through. Sometimes it is literally the sunshine, sometimes it is a call from our ALZ support group, sometimes it is a donut that I should not eat, sometimes it is a phone call, and sometimes it is just a smile or a touch. So during the course of the week, when things get difficult, or when you are wondering how long can I do this, or do I really need to visit today...just whistle this tune to yourself, I believe it will make the sun shine. And when it does, your sun will shine a little brighter for someone else.

When skies are gray, you are the sunshine of the day... "You are my sunshine, my only sunshine, You'll never know dear how much I love you, please don't take my sunshine away." You are the sunshine. But without your own sunshine you do not have it to give. So take care of the care giver as well as the patient...it is the only way the Sun can Shine!

Today would have been my mom's birthday. I miss her as much as ever...but she still makes my sun shine! That is what care givers do...they make the sun shine every day!

Hugs my friends, let's walk to end this disease on Sept. 24. Let's make the sunshine!

Enjoy your sunshine today and when the rains do come, you will be the sunshine!

Me

GM My Wonderful Support Group,

Happy Labor Day weekend! While this is a weekend to celebrate all of the world's Laborers, it is also a weekend to celebrate Caregivers/advocates, as this is truly a Labor of Love. The good news when there is Love... there is Joy! So take some time this weekend to relax and enjoy your Labor of Love.

I am thinking this weekend's weather is another wonderful reminder of our journey and any Labor of Love. Here we are set to enjoy Labor Day weekend, perhaps with special plans and then we begin hearing the news about Hermine and we try to prepare as best we can. We can only be so prepared because we really are not sure in which direction the storm is going to go. Will all of our weekend plans be ruined? We are not sure, so we prepare: we tuck away the things that may blow, take down the wind chimes as suggested on the news, some of us may even prepare for power outages, others may say this will just be wind and rain...no worries. We all face the storm in a different way, but however we face it, we prepare for what we believe is about to happen...and in most cases give it just a bit more thought than if there had been no signs of a storm at all.

Finally, the storm hits and truthfully it is windy with much-needed rain, but not nearly as bad as we thought it was going to be. We begin to wonder what all the worry was about. We handled it with no problem. We wake up to overcast skies and then slowly but surely we see more sun and we are eventually able to get out and enjoy the day. Our Labor Day plans are not ruined.

We let our guard down and believe the storm is over, crawl into bed, sleep easily, and there it is again...another huge rainstorm...but this time we do not have everything tucked away and now we are left wondering if the chairs will blow, what damage could occur and we have a sleepless night, leaving ourselves a little weaker and more vulnerable to the stress of the storm. But when we rise, it is once again a new day, all is well.

We made it! The sun will come out and in truth, we are better off, as the rain is something we truly needed. We do not always see the beauty of the storm at the moment of the storm warning, but when we wash away the debris of the storm we can see clearly that... all is well. We do not regret our preparations, we are just grateful that the storm has passed and we made it!

This is true with the Labor of Love of the caregiver. This is true with the journey of ALZ. We read, we listen, and we try to prepare for what is ahead, but we really do not know in which direction our loved one will go. We prepare as best as possible, we even breathe easy when things are going well and give thanks that it is not as bad as we thought it might be. We feel as if our Labor of Love is not a labor at all, we are happy to do all we can, and then overnight there is a change that we did not see coming. We are not quite as prepared as we thought we were, we are more tired than before, a little more exhausted and we are left wondering if we can make it through this journey. Yet, this is a Labor of Love, and our Love drives us forward. Yes, we wonder if we will be able to enjoy the holiday, we have doubts, we question ourselves...and then...when we wash away the debris, take a breath, and say that prayer, Dear Lord give me the strength...there it is...we can see clearly and we know we can do this. We may need help, we may need the support of others, but with Love we continue forward.

Sometimes we need a break from the storm...sometimes we need to wash the windows to see clearly once again...but with Breath and Love and Support and Prayer, we move forward once again and the journey is continued with LOVE.

So my friends, Happy Labor Day weekend. Today you deserve a break from your Labor of Love. Take time to enjoy this day. The sun will come out, but remember, the rains will return, we don't know when, so prepare as best you can and then just "Breathe, Pray, and Love."

Many Hugs and Much Love and Appreciation for all that YOU do,

Me

Good Morning Sunshine!

I hope that is exactly what you hear each time you walk in to see your Loved One...Good Morning Sunshine, or The Love of My Life, or There you are my Sweet Child/Baby! My mom used to say...There's my sweet Baby. (I am the baby of the family and she always said...you will always be my baby.) Those are the words that lit up my world, so I carried them in my head and said them out loud each time I walked in to see mom! From her lips, to God's ears, to my heart...what more do we need?

So today, this new day and new week, I guess I am thinking...MANTRA, PRAYER or SUNSHINE! Whatever it is that makes your heart and soul feel lighter and happier, that is what you should hear first thing every morning. So what is your SUNSHINE? What is it that brings you happiness each time you see your loved one? That is my prayer for you this week, the words that make your heart and soul feel like the morning sun rising.

110

This morning I am borrowing from my inspirational reading titled..."I Do Not Walk Alone Through Life."

I do not walk alone through life, for God is within me and around me. I am blessed and protected in all I do. Every moment carries a gift for me. May I receive it and pass it on.

I can assure you there have been moments and very long dark moments in my life journey where these words would ring a bit empty in my ears. Do I want to pass on the journey with ALZ, what gift is there in watching and caring and loving a person with ALZ? Stop right now, take a deep breath, and look all around you...do you see the love, the friendship, the family, that has carried you through your journey. It is there, right in front of you, and sometimes we cannot see it. This morning, right now, see it, breathe it in, and remind yourself of the love you have had in your life journey...it is with you always, even during the darkest hours.

Yes, sometimes it takes deep breathing and a great deal of "extra" prayer to see what we know is there..Love, Hope, Courage, Peace, Joy...all of it...it is right in front of us...we just need to take time to see it and enjoy it. Today is that day, the day to remember the Love, the HOPE, in our life journey.

I will end with what I think is the funniest and yet a simple reminder that we need to be grateful for what we have, do not take these simple life treasures for granted. NOSE HAIR! I miss my nose hair, it filters so much and yet I never once was grateful for nose hair...until now! So take time this morning to chuckle out loud, look around, and be grateful for all of those things that surround you that are life's blessings in your life journey... including your nose hair!

Much Love and Happiness today and always my friends. See you tomorrow! I cannot wait to hug each of you that has brought a smile to my face during my Life Journey!

Hugs,

Me

P.S. Remember the walk is Sept. 24, we have made such big strides in the research for a CURE, come and join us, each step is a giant leap for ALZ!

P.P.S. Joyce, I hope I made you laugh!

GM My Wonderful Care Giving Advocates,

Happy Sunday. I hope you had a moment to enjoy that beautiful full moon last night...it was absolutely gorgeous and just another reminder that this morning we have another fresh start. Our slate is not wiped clean on the first day of the week, or the month, or the year...but EVERY DAY, EVERY MOMENT is a new beginning. So let's CELEBRATE now!

Today my heart is filled with so much love from CELEBRATING life. Another day to enjoy and to appreciate the abundance of love and support we are surrounded with on a daily basis! Thank you GOD!

So, this morning, let it go. Anything that happened, the frustration you might have felt, the tears that may have rolled, the anger at the disease, LET IT GO! It is a new day and there is nothing but a FRESH start to this day in front of you, a clean slate! How lucky are we that each morning when our eyes open, it is a new day, a day to CELEBRATE life itself and the LOVE we have been blessed to enjoy over the years. This new day may even help us to appreciate what our loved ones enjoy...a fresh start every moment. What you do today will come back to you twofold...so CELEBRATE today... a new day, a fresh slate...it is yours to write on and make it what you want. It is a new moment in time...let go of the past because if you don't you may just miss the simple miracle that is unfolding right now, this moment, and it could be the very best moment in your LIFE!

So GOOD MORNING SUNSHINE...it is a NEW DAY...CELEBRATE LIFE, this moment in time! It is all yours to make it shine. What you do right this moment will be gone in a moment, so no regrets, just start fresh and make this the BEST MOMENT so far. We are so blessed with new beginnings every moment. So take a deep breath and enjoy the moment...it is your new beginning!

Love you all so much, I hope you can feel the love that surrounds you at every given moment! It will carry you through the difficult times...I promise...I know it to be true.

Many hugs and Much Love,

Me

GM Wonderful Friends,

Today is the first Sunday in October, a new month, the beginning of fall and a new week. It makes me think about the highs and lows of the past month and season. So my words this week are STRENGTH and WEAKNESS.

Sometimes during life's journey I feel so STRONG, as if every decision I make leads me in the right direction, and then all of a sudden I feel as if I am hit with one piece of bad news after another. During those difficult times, I feel WEAK and wonder what I did wrong to make this happen. I remember asking myself WHY did mom get ALZ and why was it so difficult for me to take care of her. Why am I so WEAK, while others seem to be handling this just fine? I would talk to friends who were dealing with so much more and they did not appear to be WEAK. What was wrong with me?

Then I would remember that there really is NOT an answer to that WHY question. Do you remember when your children or your grandchildren bombarded you with those "why" questions that you just couldn't answer? That is the same for us when we ask why...there is no answer. When I am feeling WEAK and chastising myself, I remember that "Jesus WEPT." He was not WEAK, but yet He wept. Right then I realize that my WEAK moments are just a part of my learning process. They make me STRONGER. They build my STRENGTH and HOPE and FAITH and TRUST in God because I realize this is just a part of life's journey and I will one day be STRONG again.

One day last week I asked a friend if I would feel old for the rest of my life, would I feel like a WEAKLING. Her reply was... "You most likely will never be able to do everything you used to do, but your faith in GOD and love for each new day will only heighten." Isn't that worth the WEAK moments in our life...to have a STRONGER passion for life itself? Perhaps that is why Jesus wept, to show us that it is a part of life's journey that gives us the STRENGTH to go forward.

So my friends, whatever you are feeling at any given time is exactly what you need to build your STRENGTH for the rest of life's journey. Accept it for what it is and know that God has YOU and He will help you through. There is no answer to why, but the journey will renew your faith and STRENGTH and we will all make it to the other side of the journey.

I would like to close with a quote from one of my readings... "Tears can come bearing the greatest gifts. Often it is our saddest moments that lead to our greatest growth." When I look back on my life's journey, I find that to be pretty accurate...even when I had doubts...I have come through STRONGER.

So lean on Him and lean on us...we are here for you during the difficult times as well as the good times. Let's celebrate TODAY, a new day, a new week, a new moment in time. BREATHE.

Hugs my Friends, enjoy the week.

Me

Good Morning My Sweet Friends,

I am sorry for the delay in writing, but yesterday was a bit hectic of a day for us as I am sure it may have been for many of you. Gary and I cut our trip short to come home and assess the damage of Hurricane Matthew. We arrived in Jacksonville late Saturday night to discover there were not any hotels available and we knew the electricity here in Palm Coast was still off, so we hotel-searched and found one available room in McClenny, FL…25 miles east of Jax. Just to give you an idea of the room, I slept on a towel in the fetal position for three hours and then told Gary that it was time to go. While it may be true that I am a bit spoiled…I promise many of you would have passed on sleeping at all. So why share all of this with you? Because once again the weather is our reminder of the ups and downs of life and the ALZ journey. Matthew has really turned our world upside down for a while, and yet while being upside down we are able to find the beauty, hope, faith, love and joy in the journey. So it is with ALZ.

First, the name Matthew is our son's name, so for him to do so much destruction is a bit personally hurtful to us, as we know our Matthew would never do such. So, our first task was to let go of the personal…have you heard that before during your ALZ journey…it is not personal, it is a disease. So our mantra…it is not personal…it is a storm. Next, we have to endure the journey, whatever that looks like for you personally, you have to ride out the storm. We happened to be in Canada, leaving Gary's brother here to take care of preparing for the storm and caring for our girls. Some of you evacuated and I imagine some of you were unable to evacuate because of your loved ones. No matter what our circumstances, we had to have a plan to…ride out the storm. The plan is so important in both of these journeys. We could not do it alone; we had to depend on Gary's brother, Lynn. Some of you depended on your church or a hotel or friends or family, no matter, you made a plan and accepted the help you needed to get through.

But as it is with the ALZ journey, it is not over, just because you made your plan and accepted the help you needed. The road to the end of the journey is long and at times it seems as if the storm will really never end. We made it home from Canada with a few bumps in the road. When we arrived in our neighborhood, we first had to drive through several water spots about 1 ½ -2 feet deep, we made it only to find that our own street was blocked with sand. We were so excited when we first turned the corner because the house and street looked great, but as we

119

ventured closer to our home we soon saw the toll Matthew took on our own personal property and that of our neighbors. We could not even get the car to our house. The electricity was off and Lynn had shut us up nicely, all hurricane shutters down...we could not get in. For 15 years we have traveled with an outdoor shutter crank, only to discover that the first time we needed it, we had left it in the garage, removing it to make room for car seats, etc. when the munchkins came to visit. By this time you are most likely saying Susan has lost it, it has been too much for her, we do not need to hear this journey. But for me, all of it is such a comparison to the journey of ALZ. There are road blocks, there are signs, there are bumps in the road, but as caregiving advocates we have to just keep on jumping the hurdle that comes from the journey.

So to bring this story to an end, we could not get into our home, the outside damage is fixable, our neighbors across the street have it much worse, so we are more blessed than many and it may appear to some, not as blessed as others. That is our choice...we determine how we choose to see the journey. While waiting for the power to return we were able to take a neighbor to Publix, purchase lunch for my brother and sister in law, go to their home, which had power, take a nap and wait for that lovely text...WE HAVE POWER!

We returned home, and thankfully Gary was able to drive close enough to the house to get the garage door opened... wahoo...we are in! On first assessment, no inward, structural damage, so GRATEFUL. Then during the night, in the quiet, I hear a small, but distinct sound that I cannot place. In search of the light thunk, I find a wet spot upstairs that was not there during our first assessment. The journey continues, it is not over, something is leaking, but overall, we are safe, the sun will come up and our home is pretty much still our haven. The small plunk will be repaired, but it is our gentle reminder that at first we cannot see all that is to come. We have to be ever vigilant and ride the storm as it comes and goes one wave at a time. Be grateful for the good news and work on making the bad news as pleasant as possible.

We love you, Matthew, despite the destruction to our daily routine, no parking in the garage for a while, finding a small leak, working in our beautiful yard for months to come, helping our neighbors as they help us, whatever the damage, it is small in comparison to the joys of life. Our beautiful Oleander tree was split in half, but beneath the broken tree are these word rocks, HOPE, FAITH, COURAGE, LOVE, and PEACE. We can make it through the storm because…IT IS NOT PERSONAL; it is just a part of life's journey.

One moment, one hour, one day at a time my friends, there is hope and love at the end of each day.

Love you, sunny skies ahead!

Me

GM Lovely Ladies,

I just saw Deana and Sandi at High Tides last night and it was a beautiful reminder of how much I miss all of you. Some of you are fortunate enough to see each other weekly at church, but there are a few of us who only have our monthly meetings to see each other and gain the support of that beautiful hug. 😊 So I miss you and look forward to our next get-together...wahoo! That brings me to my thought for this week...PEACE.

I saw Deanna just as she and Fred were leaving and we had not eaten yet...but I chased them down (you know, got up and walked to catch up with them) and wow, was it worth it...I got the best hug and felt so at PEACE. Then Sandi joined us and we had a group hug...again PEACE. I had begun thinking about the feeling of PEACE after meeting with a wonderful friend and yoga instructor on Friday and the word has been with me ever since. So PEACE is my word for the week.

My friend Debbie is traveling what I think to be one of the most difficult journeys in life, the loss of her son. It has been a little over a year now, but it was the first time we had been together since her son had died. She wrote a most beautiful tribute to his memory on the one-year anniversary and I was determined to reconnect. I am so grateful for that determination.

As we sat outside to catch up with each other's journey, you could feel it in the air, but it also was a part of our conversation...over and over...the PEACE of acceptance. The understanding that life is filled with ups and downs that we cannot understand and are not supposed to understand, but are a part of the greater picture and will lead us to where we need to be, and when we arrive we will feel the PEACE of God's hand.

We have all felt that anxiety, we have all questioned WHY, but still we believe and continue forward trusting that God has us in His hands and that He will guide us to our place of PEACE and reconciliation. So whenever there is doubt, be patient, you are not alone and the road ahead though bumpy and even down right rocky at times, is secure. God is with you, He has your hand and He will see you through.

Debbie shared with me an analogy a friend shared with her. I would like to share it with you. Her friend remembers as a small boy that his mother loved to do needlepoint, so while he played on the floor she would sit on the couch and do her needlepoint. When he would look up he would see the back of her work and it was

123

knotted and tangled and he would wonder what the purpose was (you know...WHY) in spending all that time making such a knotted mess and then...when she would finish she would call him to come look...and he would SEE the most beautiful work of art. Such is the journey of life. So be strong my friends, be at PEACE with your journey, it may be tangled at times but you are making the most beautiful work of art. Thank you for all you do for your loved ones and others.

Much love my friends and until we meet again...feel the PEACE of the journey...it is there.

Me

GM My sweet Friends and Care Giving Advocates,

Here it is the last Sunday in October...the end of the month, which brings us closer to the end of another year. I have had many thoughts about today's message...most of them came to me at 2:00 AM, but I forced myself to stay still and I did fall back to sleep eventually with the final thought of...a Chapter in a Book. The two o'clock debate was pretty long and it was between Matthew and the book...but I decided that Matthew was just a part of the Chapter and the book was a win-win situation. (Yes, it is difficult to live in my mind at times, I admit it. ☺)

So, here we are at the end of another chapter in the book of ALZ. Just like with any book, some chapters are long and tedious to get through and for me that is how October has been with the wake of the storm. Some books are an easy and enjoyable read, some are filled with mystery and suspense, some with sorrow and hardship, some with love and compassion. So too is a year in the ALZ story, the difference is the book, The Journey of ALZ is filled with all the book genres you could possibly read.

When you have a good book, one you love dearly, it is at times difficult to put down. Yet, it can also take time to get into the story...you know the first 100 pages. Then here you are so thoroughly loving this book and you come to a chapter called October...or perhaps for you 2016, and the story takes a huge turn that you just did not expect and that you just cannot believe to be true. You feel as if you are close to the end of the book and now this destructive chapter.

How could this happen? You are so angry with the author for the storm of this chapter you are not sure if you can finish the book. You close the book and do not want to even think about it for a while... the author ruined this book you loved...why? But you cannot help but think about the book, so you regain your strength to see how the story unfolds. As you begin to read chapter November, you are sure in your heart of hearts that the story will end well...because you have loved this book until this point in time. You pray that the author does not throw in any more devastating surprises, but you are not sure, you just pray for a happy ending to this book you love.

We do not yet know the end of the story...but we will...and the end will be filled with smiles and love and peace. Yet when you think about the book, you still wonder why the author threw in October, such a stormy chapter, or even the year 2016, so confusing and discombobulating. But despite those chapters, you love this book.

Such is ...The Journey of ALZ. It is difficult to understand at the beginning of the story. You wonder what is going on, who this story is about, where this story is going. You put the story down to take a breather every now and then and sure enough you make it past the first few chapters. You now understand it is about a disease, not the person, and you better understand the plot of the story.

You love this story because you love the main character in the book so much despite what the dreaded disease has done to the unfolding of the story. So you continue to read, getting support by putting it down when you just need a break and picking it back up when you are re-energized, discussing it with friends when you have the time.

Sometimes you cannot put the book down and it totally takes your breath away...you are sure you will not be able to sleep until the story ends...but you do...you fall asleep reading the book night after night. Then chapter October comes to an end and you are devastated by what just took place...the storm hit...and there is destruction everywhere. What happened to the story you loved? You set the book down, you close your eyes, you take a breath and all you can see is that beautiful main character and all the love that emanates from them. You are angry at the author for throwing you this curve ball chapter, but you still love the characters and the book...you want to finish reading the book and you will...because it is the story of a life time.

So my friends, close the book when you must, close your eyes and take a deep breath, visualize the characters in the story and all the love you feel for them, and when you open your eyes once again you will feel the desire to finish the story...you will make it to the end...despite what chapter October brought. You know the author of the story will support you to the end of the book, your love for the main character will remain strong.

Hugs my friends, the end of Oct. is near. November is around the corner and we will meet again to discuss the book...The Journey of ALZ and chapter October.

Happy Halloween,

Me

> *Dearest Susan, your Sunday messages to your ALZ support group, which you, Margo and Robin started to help all those who are caretakers dealing with parents or partners who are on their ALZ journey, are the most beautiful and meaningful inspirations! You speak from your heart and your experience! I find strength and knowledge from your wisdom! Don't know how I would have survived this trip without you, the support group, my wonderful family and God!*
> *– Judy Wiginton*

Good Morning My Wonderful Friends,

I hope that you had a wonderful week and that you were able to take a moment just to breathe each and every day. Funny how after one night of sleep it is not only a new day, but a new week. While it has been an interesting week and for many a difficult week, it is now in the past and it is time to move forward.

I have been bantering with two words this morning...CHANGE and PERSISTENCE.

Perhaps we need both of these words this week. I believe the world could use a lesson from all of you my friends, as you are witnessing a CHANGE of a lifetime. One that can take one's breath away, the CHANGE in your loved one. Honestly, what can be more difficult than that? You have been hit by Hurricane Matthew, the election, despite your candidate choice it has brought about CHANGE, and yet you do not falter, you do not burn the photos of the good moments, you do not bash cars in anger...

129

no, what you do is step up your PERSISTENCE. You love deeper, you work harder, you build your compassion, you give more...you are PERSISTENT in your caregiving. This does not mean that the CHANGE does not scare you at times, that it does not rob you of your energy. What it means is that your love is deeper than the CHANGES you see and you are PERSISTENT enough to move forward and meet the challenge head on. You are unfaltering in your love, in your kindness, in your compassion, in your willingness to make the CHANGE as beautiful as possible. Thank you for that, such a life lesson.

My courageous friends, thank you for once again showing me the miracle and beauty of the caregiving journey. It is not an easy road, all of life's up and downs continue, and yet you continue your caregiving with love and compassion. There is no time to mourn the loss of daily changes, you are on the journey of a life time and you accept the daily CHANGE you witness in your loved ones. And then through your love and PERSISTENCE you gain the strength to move forward and to survive. Not only do you survive, but you become more compassionate, more loving, more caring in your advocacy. That is the beauty of CHANGE, it makes one stronger.

Yesterday was the one-year anniversary of the death of a dear friend, my dear friend's spouse. That is a life-altering CHANGE. The day was filled with emotion and tears, yet with PERSISTENCE and kindness we forged through the day to end with the moon rising in all its glory. There was a man in the moon last night...I am sure it was Steve saying thank you for your love, for your compassion, for your kindness, for your PERSISTENCE... move forward...all will be well. Take the miracles as they come, do not let the CHANGE bring you down, take heart because you are PERSISTENT and you will not only survive, you will be better from the journey.

Hugs my dear friends, you are a role model to the world. I am grateful to each of you for life lessons in the beauty of CHANGE and PERSISTENCE. Thank you for all you do every day to make this world a better place...you are PERSISTENT in your love and kindness, your ability to give of yourself. You do not question the CHANGE you accept it!

Thank you,

Me

Good Morning My Friends,

I am so sorry that I am late with this note, but it was for a very JOYful reason...I was on a Disney Cruise with our 8 munchkins. Now talk about JOY! If the world worked as hard as Disney to keep things clean and JOYFUL...this would truly be a wonderful world! The good news of being late...it is closer to Thanksgiving...so Happy Thanksgiving to all of you.

Before I left on our cruise I was being pulled down by the weight of the world around me. I made a vow as we were leaving to return with all the JOY of the cruise and to avoid the stresses of life. Well, that is easier said than done, but my nephew shared a few words of wisdom with me..."EXPECT nothing from anyone but YOURSELF and you won't be disappointed." Where did this young man gain all of this wisdom...from life's journey. Trust me, he took a lot of hard knocks before he became this gentle and JOYFUL soul. You can see the JOY on his face every moment...it is a beautiful thing to witness.

Now why do I share this with you... my wonderful Care Givers and Advocates? I realized that at times the frustrations and impatience I felt during my journey with my mother was because I was setting expectations for her. I wanted her to remember certain things, I wanted her to shower and eat and do it when I expected it to be done. I set expectations for her instead of for myself. I realize in hindsight that it would have been much more pleasant if I just set expectations for myself...for example...I will make mom laugh and smile as much as possible....I will find something mom likes to eat today...I will ask her when she would like to shower...I will be more patient with my mom and MYSELF today...I will be JOYFUL. In truth when I look back, when I was able to do that, it was a pretty wonderful day. My husband did this every day with her...he brought her JOY because he was JOYful and did not expect anything from her. It was me who set expectations for my mom. When I let them go...it was a pretty JOYful journey.

Yes, it is so true, life itself brings stress but we have to decide to allow it to stress us or to be JOYFUL and let the stress go. ☺ Today I expect to be JOYFUL. I expect to remember the beautiful moments of the trip. I expect myself to bring the JOY of Disney to my everyday world...after all...Disney can, so can I.

To watch a ship filled with children, 8 of our own, and see nothing but JOY on their faces is an amazing thing to witness. Eight children, four from 3-11, without their parents for six days and no meltdowns...really?! Yes, REALLY. The JOY of Disney was with them on the trip...they had no expectations of what it should be like, they were not disappointed in any of it! While it is true that Disney outdid any expectations I could possibly have had...what I did notice was...the adults had meltdowns, stresses that they allowed in. No, I did not have time to view all the photos the ship took, nor did I get to purchase all the gifts I wanted...but I did get to witness JOY...unexpected JOY!

So this Thanksgiving, my dear friends, be thankful for the JOY in your heart and let it shine every day. Let JOY be your only expectation during this holiday season...your own JOY... because when your JOY shines...you will find the JOY in others. Set no expectations for your loved one, just for yourself, allow them to enjoy the quiet moment instead of the hustle and bustle of the holiday. Allow your JOY to be all the JOY they need.

Happy Thanksgiving my friends,

enJOY,

Me

GM My Wonderful Care Giving Advocates,

I hope that all of you had a wonderful Thanksgiving and that you took the day to think gratitude. What a wonderful day...a day to give thanks.

So now we are in the transition week, the last Sunday in November, and before the week ends a new month will be here. The first day of the first week of Advent. I took a moment to look up the history of Advent and these are the words set before me: hope, peace, joy and love; promise, prophecy, proclamation and presence.

When I woke up this morning, I was not thinking about the first week of Advent, but rather transition week. When I read my Daily Word and saw the first week of Advent, I realized that for me... they work beautifully together...transition and Advent. It is a time of hope, peace, joy and love. What beautiful words to look forward to all month long.

135

ADVENT sure brings back beautiful family traditions, some of which I have left behind and may bring out once again. For example, the lighting of the Advent wreath each night before dinner. Becoming of age to be able to read the prayer each night of the week. My parents took the first week, then my brother, my sister was next and then finally week four was my turn...I just had to be able to read the prayers. I remember practicing when I was five...I practiced my week of prayers every day so that it would finally be my turn. Talk about hope, peace, joy and love...that was in my heart for four weeks. While I did not realize it, the four P's were with me as well...the promise of a turn, the prophecy that my turn would come, the proclamation that it was my turn and the presence of the strength of God to guide me through the readings.

I know what you are saying...now Susan that is not at all what the four P's are about...you and your turn...but in truth, that *is* what the four P's are about. Each of us and how when we hold hope, peace, joy and love in our hearts...God will be there for us...He has told us so....He has proclaimed the mystery of faith.

I do not want to get too preachy here as I am not capable of it in truth, but what I am asking you to do this week, the first week of Advent, is to think about the transition which is taking place. Take time each morning to look back to the year and years gone by, remember with hope, peace, joy and love. Share these memories with your loved one/s. Take out those old photos of Christmas past and talk about the loving memories of each year.

Laugh and cry as you remember for your loved one/s. Do not share these memories just with the ALZ patient, but with those that love them, so they remember the way it was. And then after looking back, look forward to this first week of Advent and think about what you can do to make this a special and memorable week for your loved one/s. What can you do, share, that will give everyone something to hold onto, to remember as the most beautiful time of the year...the promise of what is to come...peace, love, joy and yes hope...for our future. Though we do not know what it will bring, there is hope of a brighter tomorrow.

What a joyous season we have entered. May the beauty of this season bring you patience, may you recall all of the loving memories of the years past, may you look forward with hope of the peace that lies ahead. May you return an old tradition or begin a new one...something to be remembered by your loved ones in the years ahead. It is you who brings the peace, love, joy and hope to your loved one...thank you...you have made this a year to be remembered with your daily words of kindness and compassion. While there may be moments that you feel impatient, in truth, it is all the moments of gentle love and joy that have made the difference.

Enjoy the transition of the season...enjoy the first day of Advent.

Many hugs and much love,

Me

GM My Sweet Care Giving Advocates,

Can you believe it is already the first week of December, that Christmas is just 21 days away? It is amazing to me how every year I know exactly when Christmas will arrive, yet it seems to get here so quickly...it is a year away every year...but it just jumps up and arrives and I seem to be caught unprepared and by surprise that it is already December! Yet here it is, and in truth, this year, I am grateful that it has arrived. I am no more prepared, but I am a bit more grateful for its arrival.

That is how I feel about the journey with ALZ. We know it is there, yet we are constantly surprised when a change, a significant change happens. We hear about it, yet we are sure it will not happen to our loved one, that it is a year or more away, and then when it does arrive, we are just surprised at its arrival. Caught unprepared even though we started thinking about it in July, we are amazed that it is already Dec., that it is the end of a year/phase and the beginning of a new year/phase is soon upon us.

138

The good news of all of this is that there is no need for despair. If we look back to all of our Decembers, no matter how surprised we were by its arrival, or how unprepared we felt when we realized it was December...we have always made it through to another December. And so here we are...the first week in December. Again, so it is true with the ALZ journey. While your heart may break over the change, or you feel a heavy burden, or an unbelievable sadness that you are surprised by, the truth is you will make it to the next day, to the next week, to the next month, to the next stage, because you my friend are an AMAZING CAREGIVER!

November has been filled with news from caregivers, surprised by the changes they see. Some have been quick, some have been a long time coming, but it does not matter, the truth is we are always caught by surprise when it happens, unprepared, so to speak. Because my friends, are we ever really prepared for the full circle of life? We know it is coming, but just like Dec., it is here before you realize it.

Today I would like you to take a moment to welcome Ginny to our group. She is a long distance group member, in Chicago, and traveling the ALZ journey with her dad. She spends some time in Palm Coast and heard of our wonderful group through Gail. She has reached out to us and I have added her to our e-mail list. So if you would like to send her your support, please feel free, just be sure to put ALZ in the subject line.

I would also like to request that we send up special prayers for my dear friend Mandi who lives in GA. She has been taking care of her mother for many years and her mom is drawing near to the end of the journey. As all of us, Mandi, while not surprised, is still not ready. Please pray for a peaceful journey for both Mandi and her mom.

And finally, please pray for my friend Joanne. She has just moved her husband into a new home, and while it is such a blessing, we all know the difficulty of that move. Deep breaths, sweet friend, all will be well.

And so, my friends, we have turned the page of November and are opening a new chapter in the book of life with ALZ. We made it to December, but what a surprise that it is already here. Take a deep breath, look back through the year and remember all that you have done, think about where you have been, let go of what you can no longer use, and enjoy the beauty of this very moment in time. It is truly all we have. Do not be afraid to reach out for help, as my t-shirt says...NO ONE FIGHTS ALONE. We are here for you!

Much love and joy for this holiday season. You are truly a blessing to all.

Me

Good Morning Ladies,

Holidays are always a special time, but we all know that they can cause anxiety and stress, as well as joy and beauty. This is one of the things I think about now that mom has gone. For four years, each holiday, especially Thanksgiving until Christmas, caused me a great deal of anxiety and stress because I did not know how mom would react. One thing I have, which is both a blessing and a curse, is...HIGH EXPECTATIONS. During my journey with ALZ, I learned the real meaning of HIGH EXPECTATIONS...have them ONLY for yourself...as You are the only one and only thing you have any control over...and even that is limited. ☺

So, my friends, I share this with you for one reason...let it GO, and let GOD. Make your plans, do not fret about them, "what will be, will be, the future is not ours to see." Now that you have made your plans, relax and enjoy the ride, just don't place expectations on anyone else but yourself and make your

141

expectation one of enjoyment. The day may look different than before, it may feel different than last year, but it is the present and if you live in that moment, you will find the beauty of the new day.

My inspirational prayer this morning is for those who have left this earth, but for ALZ it is true long before then, because in many ways our loved ones have left us long before they have left this earth. You all know...perhaps it is the phone calls, or the holding hands, or just sitting together, whatever is missing, you already miss, so I think this prayer is appropriate for all of us...

"May God fill my heart with an inner knowing that those who have left have not left at all, for they remain in His heart and in mine. I feel peace as I remember them, for I know they are not gone. May they, and I rest peacefully in the arms of God."

So this holiday season, rest peacefully in the arms of God, enjoy the moment with your loved one, whether they are with you or gone in some way, shape or form. For it is that love and expectation of self that will bring you joy in the holiday season and each day to come.

Hugs my dear friends.

Happy Holidays,

Me

Good Morning Fabulous Ladies,

Today is Sunday, a new day and a new week. Sometimes it is difficult to believe we are just weeks away from a NEW YEAR! Can you remember what was happening a year ago today? Wow, the difference a year can make.

I do not know where you are in the spirit of Christmas, but - we started early this year, as there seemed to be a lot to be done in early Dec. I had three different parties to attend last week, so the spirit of Christmas just seemed to arrive early this year and I guess we took advantage of that spirit. Our Christmas tree has been up since Dec. 1. I love the early mornings with the lights twinkling in the quiet of the rising sun. It makes me feel peaceful and prayerful.

Well, yesterday that beautiful sparkling tree decided to come tumbling down, yep, just fell right over, taking out a number of precious ornaments and decorations. For one fleeting moment I thought...I am going to cry...but then a calm came over me and I just went about cleaning up the mess. While cleaning up and un-decorating what was left, I thought for another fleeting moment...I am just going to throw this tree out and forget about sparkling lights...and then I just worked on getting the tree in a better

143

position to remain standing...hopefully, for the rest of the season. So this morning there she is in all her glory, a few less ornaments, but clearly straighter and stronger in her stance and sparkling as brightly as before her fall.

As I sat down to write to you this morning I realized how much that reminded me of your daily journey. One moment all is well and then...in a split second, disaster has knocked on your door. In a split second you have to respond and in that second you have to make a decision. It is your choice: you can get upset and toss the tree out...or just begin cleaning up the mess and get back to enjoying the sparkling moments of life.

Here is a quote I read this morning, I think it is so appropriate for all of us, but especially during the journey of ALZ.

"It's a decision I make every morning when I wake up. I have a choice;

I can spend the day in bed recounting the difficulty I have with the parts of my body that no longer work, or get out of bed and be thankful for the ones that do.

Each day is a gift, and as long as my eyes open, I'll focus on the new day and all the happy memories I've stored away. Just for this time in my life.

Old age is like a bank account. You withdraw from what you've put in.

So, my advice to you would be to deposit a lot of happiness in the bank account of memories!"

144

So my dear Caregivers, it is your choice how each day unfolds. While it is not fair that ALZ is a part of our life journey, it is, and we can choose to make beautiful memories or just give up and never see the sparkling lights again. While it is true, that at times that choice seems to be such a heavy burden, in truth, it is a split-second decision, a simple prayer, sometimes more of a plea, that can turn the lights on once again or leave you standing in the dark.

So during this Advent Season, fill up that bank account of life and take time to enjoy the sparkling lights of life, whenever they come. Make a choice to make it work, however that looks for you at this moment in time.

Hugs my friends, we will be together tomorrow to share and support and cherish, it is our choice.

Me

> *Susan, I came to know you when I was so low! Our little morning coffees with Margo gave me the strength and the motivation to keep going and caring for my dear Mama. When we decided to open up our group and start "Hope in the Hammock," a whole new world opened up. Sharing and caring with others in our same situation was and continues to be so precious, so rewarding. I thank God every day for you, dear Susan. You are truly an angel on Earth. Thank you so much for your inspirational letters. I treasure every one.*
> *– Robin Sullivan*

GM My Favorite Rays of Sunshine!

'Tis the season for celebrating! Isn't it amazing how such a JOYFUL time can also be such a STRESSFUL time! So much to ENJOY we stress ourselves out. Every year I say I am not going to STRESS this year...but somehow it just does not seem to happen. But what I have been able to do is remember to take better care of my self during this harried Season of JOY and LOVE. So these are my thoughts and prayers for you as you traverse the holiday season during your ALZ journey. These simple tips are good for all of us and especially for those with ALZ.

The first thing I want you to remember... take it slow and easy. Doesn't that sound simple? 😊 So easy to say... not so easy to do. But there are simple tricks to help you slow your pace...remember...BREATHE. Think of Gail and the breathing exercises she shared...simple, just a matter of minutes, but some deep BREATHS will slow you down for sure...so #1 on my list is take time to BREATHE!

146

Next on my list, KEEP IT SIMPLE SILLY... "KISS." Do the things you really enjoy about the holiday...put out the decorations you love, bake the goodies that are your favorite, go to the places you really want to go...if it is not something you love to do...just don't do it. Simple, really! And for your LOVED ones with ALZ, do NOT make them be a part of something that will only add stress to your holiday and theirs. Think of memories past that can be shared and talked about...remember for them. KISS!

If you have a sadness or heavy heart, give yourself PERMISSION to acknowledge and accept that feeling. Take time to mourn your loss. Wash your soul with your tears so that you will be able to move forward with the JOY of the season.

Finally REMEMBER... what the season is truly about, why we celebrate CHRISTMAS. Once you focus on what the REASON for the SEASON is...the rest is nothing but icing on the cake. Taking time to focus on why we are celebrating CHRISTMAS will open your heart to the miracle of the season. It will fill you with JOY and you will be nothing but GRATEFUL for the journey of LIFE. Yes, even with all of its ups and downs you will feel GRATEFUL.

So my friends, TIS the SEASON to celebrate LIFE. Remember the beautiful moments, LEARN from the difficult times, and CELEBRATE this moment in time. CHERISH it as it is, this moment is all we have, so make the most of it.

You are loved, you are NOT alone and YOU are making a difference in the world around you.

Merry Christmas my friends and I hope to see you tomorrow as we take a moment to celebrate each other.

Love you all,

Me

GM My Sweet and Caring Advocates,

We are one week away from Christmas and two weeks away from beginning a brand New Year! Wow! 'Tis the Season of "Comfort and Joy!"

So Comfort and Joy are our words to focus on this morning. There is much during this time of year that can bring us Comfort and Joy: holiday decorations, baking, family, doing for others, parties, songs, festivities galore and ummm, some really lovely COMFORT foods. 😊 Yet those very things... besides bringing us COMFORT and JOY... can actually cause us stress. Especially when dealing with the illness of a loved one as difficult as ALZ. At times unpredictable, to say the least.

It is such a fine line between Comfort and Joy and stress. What makes the difference? It is US...it is how we choose to see it, it is what we make of it...it is US. So easy, yet so difficult.

I am the first to admit that there have been times, and yesterday was one of them, that I have walked away and said to Gary...they zapped the Joy right out from under this experience.

And then when I have had time to put my feet up, take that deep BREATH, and relax and meditate on the moment of Joy...I realize it is my choice whether or not I let "them" zap the JOY right out of the moment.

With the ALZ journey there are so many unknowns. We have no real idea of what Christmas morning will bring...but you can take this week to make sure that the day brings you COMFORT and JOY. How? By thinking about you and your loved one and what would make you feel good, despite the disease. I learned from my mother's journey with ALZ and now my own journey with cancer that I have to be able to say, if possible... we will be there. I do not put stress on myself to make it happen. And if we cannot be there...then I have to find something that will make the moment full of COMFORT and JOY despite the change in plans.

For some of you it will be a short and loving visit with your loved one...enjoy it and then enjoy the rest of your day...GUILT-free. If you are the full-time care giver and will spend the day with your loved one, be mentally prepared that you may need to make changes and accept them, do not let those changes zap your JOY. Have plan B prepared that will make it a lovely day no matter what.

So here is my example. One Mother's Day I had flowers and a brunch prepared for my mother. She woke up in a great mood and then a caretaker arrived to help her shower and dress while I got ready. She had a meltdown...the day was over and I was disappointed. When I look back, it was all my fault. Did I really need to have someone come and help her shower...no. Did she have to get dressed to make it a great Mother's Day...no. All that really mattered was that we were together, but I wanted more. The next holiday I was prepared. I took the day as it came. I took total charge of what she wanted to do to get ready. No shower... ok. Would you like to wear this...great. Would you like to go out or stay home...choice. I was prepared for whatever answer came...I had plans to give us both Comfort and Joy no matter what the day brought.

So my friends...you are in charge of your own COMFORT and JOY. Do not let anything zap it from you. Put on the Christmas music, bake your favorite comfort foods even if just for yourself, sing and Deck the Halls with nothing but Comfort and Joy. Reminisce, make plans for the New Year and all the Joy you will find in the small sparkling miracles of each and every day. They are there, we just have to open our hearts to them...let the real REASON for the SEASON fill your heart with Comfort and Joy and know that you are not alone, you are loved and you will have a wonderful Christmas. A Christmas that you will remember forever...because no one can zap your Comfort and Joy...you are the Comfort and Joy of this Christmas season.

Yes, I have the Christmas lights on, the candles lit, the music playing, I am set for a JOYFUL day...I will make my own

JOY, I will keep my heart full of love and when that light shines on others it will come back to me twofold. Enjoy your loved one, however the day unfolds, find the JOY of that moment. The best choice...no pressure...just Comfort and JOY.

Merry, Merry Christmas my friends. I wish you a week of nothing but Comfort and Joy.

Hugs,

Me

Merry Christmas my sweet Care Giving Friends,

May you find Peace and Joy in the celebration of Christ's birth this morning. Feel His love and strength all around YOU throughout this day and relax in that LOVE. No expectations, just simple Joy and Love.

Merry Christmas my sweet friends. It is a beautiful morning. Put on the Christmas music, light the holiday candles and just enjoy the celebration of the day.

Much Love and Many Hugs,

Me

Happy New Year my wonderful FRIENDS,

Keep your eyes, ears and heart open because today is an amazing day. A new moment in time, a new day, the first day of the new week, the first day of the new month, and the first day of the New Year! Wow, it cannot get much better than this moment to let go of what we cannot change and start fresh with nothing but faith, hope and promise. Happy New Year!!!

I want to begin with a quote from an early onset ALZ gentleman who had an article in the ALZ Assoc. newsletter. He was about to celebrate his first Christmas with ALZ. I found it to be a wonderful reminder to all of us. Here is what he said: "Alzheimer's may have changed my brain's biology, my personality and my expressions, but I tell my family that the essence of who I am in my heart remains the same." Wow...The essence of who I am in my heart remains the same. What kind and gentle words to begin this wonderful day. Please let this resonate in your heart and on your tongue when you are speaking with family members or young ones...*the essence of what is in my heart remains the same*...the heart is who we want to remember. I love that.

Next, my friend Mandi, whom you met through these letters, sent me the title of a book that she found very powerful. I have not yet finished the book, but am halfway through and I see why it is so helpful for caregivers. The title is "Precious Lord, Take My Hand" by Shelly Beach. I know you are saying Susan, where will I find the time to read. But remember it is a new day filled with wonderful potential. This is not a book that you must read in one seating. Each few pages will give you a prayer to carry you forward and perhaps the strength you need for the day.

So when you have a moment, you may just want to check it out. I downloaded it on my Kindle, but I am thinking it is most likely in our library. My favorite parts are the prayers, as they are stated in a way I would never have thought to pray during my journey. It will remind you that you are not alone, to seek help from others and possibly bring great purpose to your journey as a caretaker. Also, on this wonderful day my friends, some words that I found to be very comforting and helpful from our friend Gail. Not only does she teach us to breathe, but she helps us let go of what we cannot control. Remember these wonderful words... "close a door and open a window"... well, Gail helped me to picture that so well. Sometimes as we walk through the door and we are beginning to close the door, it is difficult to let go of the door knob....we may tend to hold on... for dear life...making it difficult to get over to the window.

So today, this new day, this New Year, this moment right now...let go of the knob and open the window so that you can BREATHE! (Of course, Gail said this much more eloquently, but hopefully I was able to give you a vision.) My friend Joanne did this in the past few months and I could see the gentle breeze from the open window blowing on her entire body, it was so refreshing to witness... you too can open the window, just let go of what you cannot control or can no longer handle alone...Breathe, and slowly open the window, enjoy and savor the breeze.

And one last final quote from the Daily Word I receive. "This new year holds within it the promise of love, joy, health, prosperity, harmony, and so much more." So thankful for this New Year, this new beginning, Today. It took me all this time, but I realize my weekly words to you...actually come from YOU. Thank you my friends, I pray for all of us to have a year filled with Love, Joy, Health, Prosperity, Harmony and so much more. Happy New Year!

Inspired by YOU, with much Love and Gratitude,

Me

Susan has been an angel on earth for so many people that it would be impossible to list all the ways she has made major differences in these lives.

Speaking only for myself, she was introduced to me by a caring friend when I was walking a difficult path with my husband, who was by then in the late stages of Alzheimer's. Susan had already walked that painful path with her mother and was able to make suggestions not only about memory care facilities, but also about taking care of myself, as well as hints about how to deal with the constantly changing challenges I would be facing.

Robin Sullivan began joining our luncheon meetings while she was going through similar experiences with her mother, who also had Alzheimer's. We found that simply being able to share our concerns, frustrations, fears, and feelings of guilt with those who had been down a similar path was profoundly encouraging. Susan was living proof that there is life after Alzheimer's, and it was during one of these episodes of sharing that we realized there must be others who would benefit from what we had experienced.

Our Alzheimer's Support group was born. Our motto was "A shared burden is a lighter burden." How true that has turned out to be.

Even beyond the counseling and support and encouragement Susan offered me, she and her husband came to my rescue after my husband transitioned to Heaven. I needed to empty his room immediately and they took pieces of furniture that they knew a specific person had a need for. They also took my husband's clothes to a local program that helped young men in recovery to dress for success in finding a job.

Mere words cannot express the love and admiration I feel for Susan and her dedication for helping others.
– Margo Usher

Team Hope in the Hammock

on the Walk to End Alzheimer's!

ABOUT THE EDITOR

Nancy Shohet West is a Boston-area journalist who helps individuals, multi-generational families, communities, and special interest groups to write and self-publish their memoirs. For more information, go to www.NancyShohetWest.com.

91851612R00096

Made in the USA
Columbia, SC
21 March 2018